Hamlyn all-colour paperbacks

H. T. Lenton

Warships

**illustrated by David A. Warner
& Nigel W. Hearn**

Hamlyn · London
Sun Books · Melbourne

FOREWORD

To encompass within one small volume the evolution of warship design since steam and iron were first adopted in about 1860 naturally means that only the most significant changes can be noted and illustrated. Selecting these significant points is made no easier by their appearance at different times in different navies; and if the first example of each new design were chosen, then the choice would be narrowed to only a few major navies. Rather than do this, the widest possible national coverage was given to the warships illustrated, but at the same time the development was kept in chronological order; this explains the anomalies which occasionally arise when a particular ship is followed by one which was built before it. Since construction time could vary from one to eight years it is more relevant to quote the date a ship was laid down rather than the date of its completion. This procedure is adhered to in the text, but in the captions, where the ships are shown in their completed state, the date is that of completion.

The types of warships have necessarily been restricted to battleships and battlecruisers, seaplane and aircraft carriers, cruisers, torpedo boats and destroyers, submarines, and gunboats and sloops, together with a collection of interesting vessels which show that warship design was not stereotyped but was frequently punctuated by examples of original thought.

H.T.L.

Published by The Hamlyn Publishing Group Limited
London · New York · Sydney · Toronto
Hamlyn House, Feltham, Middlesex, England
In association with Sun Books Pty Ltd Melbourne

Copyright © The Hamlyn Publishing Group Limited 1970

ISBN 0 600 00284 5
Phototypeset by Filmtype Services Ltd., Scarborough
Colour separations by Schwitter Limited, Zurich
Printed in England by Sir Joseph Causton & Sons Limited

CONTENTS

INTRODUCTION

Warship design, practically unchanged for four hundred years, underwent complete transformation during the mid-nineteenth century with the introduction of steam and iron. The latter had the greater influence, but it was the combination of both that resulted in drastic changes in design.

In its final stage the sailing warship fell into well-defined groups: the ship-of-the-line, frigate, corvette, sloop, gunboat, and the flotilla of inshore vessels. Their complement was determined then, as now, by the numbers required to man the armament. The main armament was the muzzle-loading, smooth-bore gun, truck-mounted on the broadside, an inaccurate weapon of limited range. These guns were carried on two or three decks in the ship-of-the-line, an enclosed main-deck in the frigate, and the open upper-deck in other vessels.

Steam and side paddle-wheels did little to alter design except reduce the number of guns that could be carried on the broadside. Since early steam engines were uneconomic, coal consumption was high and the full rig had to be retained for cruising under sail; steam was raised only in an emergency or when action was imminent. Early steam was unpopular: it increased the fire risk, and there was no denying the vulnerability of paddle-wheels to gunfire. However this last obstacle was met by the introduction of screw propulsion, which could be placed below the water-line, and with it the retention of steam was assured.

The next significant step was with ordnance, when shell supplanted solid shot. The resulting clamour to keep out shell led to the provision of iron protective plating secured externally to the wooden hull. As most of this protection was placed above the water-line (and hence above a ship's centre of gravity), it could not be extended above the lower-deck of a ship-of-the-line owing to the top weight involved; this resulted in the abandonment of the second and third gun-decks which, for so long, had been the main distinguishing feature of these vessels.

Two other factors which profoundly affected warship design were the turret system of mounting guns and guns of much increased size. The mobility imparted by steam had

The British battleship *Agincourt* was completed in 1867; all guns were carried on the broadside.

clearly shown the inflexibility of the broadside system of mounting guns: they had such small arcs of training that the ship often had to be turned to bring the guns to bear. If this new mobility was to be fully utilized then guns had to bear on all points of the horizon, and the system evolved was to mount them on turntables. The great drawback was the need to carry a full rig whose masts and rigging severely restricted the clear arcs provided by the turret system; it was not until steam propulsion was sufficiently reliable to dispense with the full rig that the turret system could be incorporated to full advantage.

The adoption of steam naturally resulted in it being used for auxiliary purposes as well as main propulsion. The gun, whose size had been restricted because it was worked manually, could now grow to the practical limits permitted by power operation. The prime object was not to increase the range but to throw a heavier projectile of greater penetrative and destructive power now that armour was being used.

In practice armour proved more resistant, when applied in sufficient thickness, than theoretical tests on the proving ground had shown. This resulted in alternative methods of attack against the unarmoured portion of the hull, and started a far-reaching cycle of development that added mines and torpedoes to the naval arsenal. Heavier guns meant that fewer

Fore-deck of the British battleship *Barfleur*, completed in 1894

The British mine counter-measure support ship *Abdiel* (1967)

could be mounted, and although they were more naturally suited to the turret system, they continued to be carried on the broadside but were grouped amidships, since to load the ends with concentrated weights would have affected seaworthiness.

There now remained one step to complete the transition from a wood-and-sail navy to one of steam and iron, and that was to build the hull itself of iron. This bold step was taken by the Royal Navy in 1859 when it laid down the *Black Prince* and *Warrior*.* The immediate result was a longer and faster ship, better able to withstand the racking strains imposed by concentrated weights. A full rig was still carried, the sole affinity to the passing era of 'wooden walls', but the foundations had been laid for the changes of the next hundred years.

*On every occasion, for 'Royal Navy' read 'British Royal Navy'.

CAPITAL SHIPS

The broadside ship *Warrior*

The title of first armoured sea-going ship fell to the British *Warrior*, although the French *Couronne* was laid down earlier.

Her design was cast around the need to carry forty 68-pounder truck-mounted guns in a partially-armoured battery. Her armament was modified before completion when the truck guns were replaced by pivoted slides which were able to train through an arc of about twenty-five degrees. This was again altered owing to the availability of the 110-pounder Armstrong breech-loading gun, and four were mounted on each side amidships in place of a pair of 68-pounders. The upper-deck chase guns – one forward and one aft – were also replaced by 110-pounders. As completed, therefore, she was armed with eight 110-pounder breech-loading smooth-bore guns and twenty-six 68-pounder muzzle-loading smooth-bore guns on the main-deck, and two 100-pounder guns on the upper-deck. The main belt was 213 feet long and extended 16 feet above, and 6 feet below, the water-line, was closed at each end by armoured bulkheads, and formed of $4\frac{1}{2}$-inch iron on 18-inch wood backing.

The hull had a clipper stem and measured 380(pp)* $\times$ $58\frac{1}{4}$ $\times$ 26 feet with a displacement of 9,210 tons.

*See page 156 for this and other abbreviations.

The revolutionary *Monitor*

While the *Warrior* was typical of the sea-going, armoured ship of the period, her design was not outstandingly original. She was a marked step forward, but only her greater length readily distinguished her from wood-and-sail counterparts.

The outbreak of the American Civil War in 1861 soon found the Federal Navy in a precarious position owing to the rapid conversion of the former frigate *Merrimack* into the Confederate ironclad *Virginia*. An immediate counter to the *Virginia* was required, and the Federals were fortunate in that the

(*Above*) cross-section of the American *Monitor* (1862) and (*below*) the Swedish monitor *John Ericsson* (1866)

These illustrations show the development of the breastwork monitor in the British Royal Navy from the low freeboard *Cyclops* of 1877 (*above*) to the *Dreadnought* of 1879 (*below*).

Swedish engineer Ericsson contracted to provide in one hundred days a vessel able to engage the *Virginia* on equal terms. She therefore had to be small for rapid construction and shallow draught, and invulnerable to existing ordnance. As her size ruled out an extensive battery, Ericsson resolved his problem by adopting the turret system and by reducing free-board, the space between water-line and deck, to 2 feet: the minimum side area was exposed with maximum protection.

When completed, the historic *Monitor* – as revolutionary as the *Warrior* was evolutionary – had an armoured raft body which overhung the shipshape hull secured below, and a single central turret mounting two 11-inch Dahlgren muzzle-loading smooth-bore guns. The *Virginia*'s broadside comprised six guns firing through narrow ports so that they could be brought to bear only by manoeuvring the ship, whereas the *Monitor*'s guns had all-round fire from the revolving turret.

The breastwork monitor

The merits of the monitor were not lost on the Royal Navy but her lack of seaworthiness did not commend her, as British policy was not one of coast defence. However, as this was a period in which British naval strength had declined, the coast defence ship was forced on the navy as an economic substitute for sea-going, armoured vessels.

In 1862 Laird, commercial shipbuilders, laid down a pair of turret ships for the Confederate States Navy which had 6-foot freeboard amidships, were fully rigged, and had a fo'c'sle and poop for sea-going service. They clearly demonstrated the incompatibility of turrets and a full rig, for not only were their clear arcs restricted by rigging but the axial fire was completely masked by the end structures.

Five years later Reed, the British chief naval architect, adapted the best features of the monitor, plus an armoured breastwork, to create a coast defence ship for colonial navies. Turrets were fitted at each end of the breastwork, and, carried $10\frac{1}{2}$ feet above the water-line, they had a better command.

The breastwork monitor was steadily developed until steam was efficient enough to be employed in sea-going ships; at this point the fully-rigged ship with its alternative method of mounting guns gave way to the turret system.

The central battery ship
The battleship was developing along two courses: on the one hand the high-sided, fully-rigged sea-going ship still carrying

The Dutch turret ram *Schorpioen*
(1869)

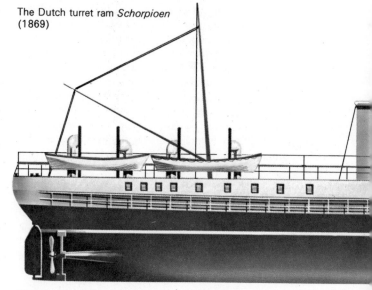

guns on the broadside; and on the other the low-sided, un-rigged coastal service vessel using the turret system.

As guns became larger, fewer could be carried on the broadside, and they were grouped amidships where the hull could best support their weight. The partial belt of the *Warrior* had been replaced by a complete belt intended both to preserve floatation at the water-line and to protect the battery. With the guns now grouped amidships, the upper part of the belt had only to cover the short central battery and was protected against raking fire by athwartship bulkheads, while the lower part still ran from end-to-end along the water-line. To improve axial fire the sides forward and aft of the central battery were recessed, and the battery was later made two-storeyed.

The turret ram

In 1866 the Austro-Hungarian and Italian fleets engaged off Lissa and gave prominence to the ram as an offensive weapon; with its end-on approach and axial fire, it was to bedevil warship design into the 1900s. For a while the ram was thought superior to the gun until fleet manoeuvres showed that there

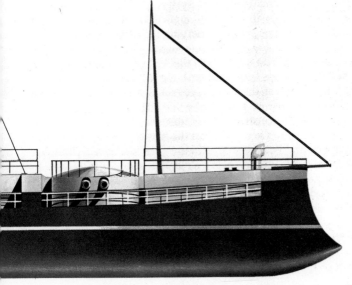

were inherent difficulties in ramming a ship on the move.

As an effective ram a ship had to have a small turning circle; this meant she had to be short and small. A single turret forward to keep the enemy under fire while closing the range was thought sufficient, and the resulting turret ram emerged as a coast defence ship and was naturally not rigged. For small navies unable to afford capital units, the turret ram proved most popular and many examples were built.

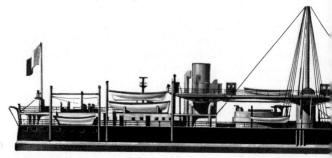

The masted turret ship

The advocates of the turret system pressed their claim in advance of their time. When applied to low-freeboard coast defence ships there was no denying the advantage of the turret system. But it was a different matter – as already explained – when applied to sea-going ships of high freeboard with all the impedimenta associated with the full rig.

The weight of the turret prevented it from being carried high, and to reduce freeboard while maintaining a full spread of canvas was constructionally unsound: and so it proved. In 1866 the Royal Navy laid down the *Monarch*, which in essence was a central battery ship with the guns carried a deck higher in two turrets and freeboard amidships reduced to 14 feet. In the next year she was followed by the *Captain* with the turrets wider spread and the superstructure angled to improve their arcs but with only $8\frac{1}{2}$-foot freeboard amidships. Unfortunately, excess weights decreased the *Captain*'s freeboard by a further 2 feet and in 1870, only six months after completion, she capsized and sank in heavy weather in the Bay of Biscay.

As a result of this tragedy the turret system received a temporary setback, but the British *Devastation* – laid down only a year after the *Captain* – heralded the abolition of masts and yards and the universal acceptance of the turret. An upward development of the breastwork monitor, the *Devastation* could stow 1,800 tons of coal and had a radius of 4,700 miles at 10 knots: a range that was more than adequate for the distances involved between coaling stations.

The Italian *Dandolo* of 1882 (*above*) and the British *Inflexible* of 1881 (*below*) were typical of the short-lived turret ship.

The mastless turret ship

The development of the battleship was forced by the advancement of ordnance: guns steadily increased in size, not so much for range as for calibre.

In the early 1870s, however, Italy saw French naval power in the Mediterranean as a threat to her security and, unable to match the French ship-for-ship, decided to build fewer units of much greater power. The Italian chief naval architect, Brin,

(*Above*) the open barbette ship *Royal Sovereign* (1892) and (*below*) the closed barbette vessel *Jauréguiberry* (1896)

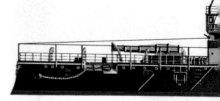

first cast his design around the 15-inch, 50-ton gun, and later recast it to adopt the 17·7-inch, 100-ton gun.

As such ships would hardly pass unchallenged, protection had to be provided against equivalent gunfire, and this was the crux of the problem. The armour required was so thick it could be provided for only a short length amidships, and

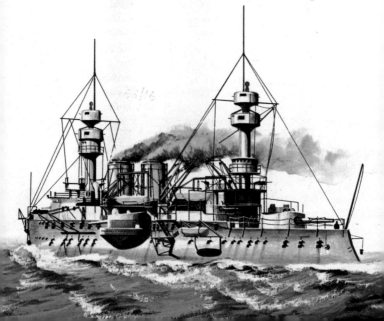

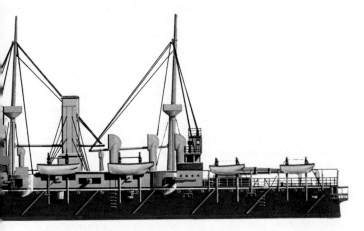

within this single citadel were grouped the vitals – the boilers, machinery, and magazines. Consequently the turrets also had to be placed amidships, and to secure the best possible all-round fire they were mounted in echelon so that four guns could bear in all directions. Outside the citadel protection was limited to submerged deck armour extending to the ends.

The *Dandolo* and *Duilio* were laid down to these specifications in 1873 with a speed of 15 knots that few other battle-ships could match. Their muzzle-loading guns were so long that special arrangements had to be made to load them from outside the turret, and this hastened the general adoption of the breech-loader. It was the torpedo threat rather than size and cost that restricted the building of these vessels.

The barbette ship

The main advantage of mounting guns in barbettes instead of turrets was that they could be carried higher; unobstructed vision enabled them to be laid and trained more easily, and there were no practical limitations on elevation and training.

The barbette was a fixed breastwork and the attraction of the system was heightened by the general return to breech-loading guns, brought about by the use of a slow-burning powder which required a long chase – impractical with a muzzle-loader – to develop its sustained pressure.

Thereafter, the simple difference between the barbette and the turret became more confused. First, bullet-proof shelters were provided at the rear of the barbette to protect the loading numbers, and these were later extended to the whole gun-crew by an open shield. Then, instead of the barbette terminating at the upper-deck, it dropped down to the main-deck to connect directly with the central citadel. Later still, the single citadel arrangement was abandoned and the main gun positions forward and aft became separate armoured stations. The need for higher speed – as explained below – resulted in increased freeboard, and the extra height meant that only the crown of the barbette now projected above the upper-deck, although there was no reduction in the height of the guns above the water-line. Heavier plating was next applied to the open gun shields, and when the rear was plated in, the position was like a half-height turret superimposed

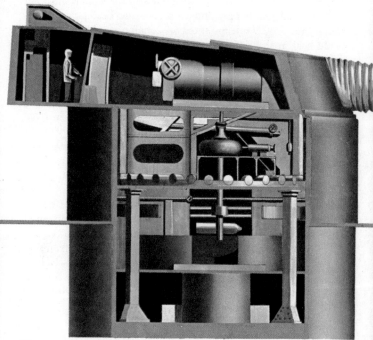

over a barbette. By general usage the turret now implied the revolving – and barbette the fixed – armoured structure.

With only part of the ship's hull armoured, a secondary armament of medium calibre guns was introduced to attack the unprotected ends. As the range was still short the open barbettes were vulnerable to attack from light guns placed high, and so small calibre guns were also incorporated. The rapid development of the medium calibre quick-firer further aggravated the problem of unarmoured ends and therefore thin armoured belts were placed along the water-line forward and aft.

But it was the torpedo that posed the greatest difficulty and, at times, threatened the very existence of the battleship between the 1880s and 1900s. An immediate passive counter was to spread an anti-torpedo net round the ship; a second was greater mobility and speed, and a third the introduction

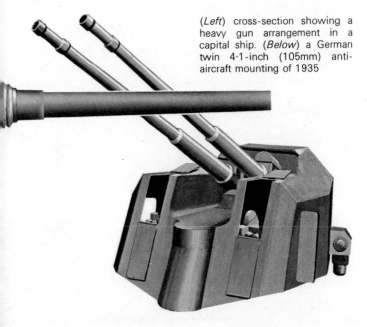

(*Left*) cross-section showing a heavy gun arrangement in a capital ship. (*Below*) a German twin 4·1-inch (105mm) anti-aircraft mounting of 1935

19

of a tertiary battery of guns to drive off all torpedo boats before they closed within range. Later, a higher degree of compartmentation and longitudinal anti-torpedo bulkheads was worked into the hull and, with development, proved a positive step. It is now evident that the torpedo threat was overrated, but one fact was established: hereafter the close blockade of an enemy coast by capital units was ruled out.

Battleship design had now reached a stage of some complexity, and the secondary armament steadily increased, both in number and in calibre, so that most of the upper-deck space was taken up with turrets. With space at a premium, superimposed turrets were introduced by the United States Navy as an alternative to siting them all at deck level, and the 'Kearsarge' class had their secondary turrets, containing two 8-inch guns, mounted on top of the twin 13-inch turrets.

The dreadnought battleship
The 1890s at last saw progress with the control of gunfire; it had long been supposed that close action was the only course open to hostile fleets. As the main guns could range to distances far in excess of that fixed for battle practice, to lengthen the range was a long overdue step.

With a satisfactory rangefinder made available, corrections were applied by spotting the fall of shot. This would be easier

(*Above*) the American dreadnought battleship *Michigan* (1910). (*Below*) the British prototype *Dreadnought* (1906)

if there were more main guns: the existing two-gun salvoes (from four main guns) were inadequate and four-gun salvoes considered minimal. Doubling the main armament would have inevitably resulted in much increased size and cost, and therefore special efforts were made to limit growth.

The first vessel of this type, the British *Dreadnought*, was rushed to completion in one year. She carried ten 12-inch guns in five twin turrets, and to secure the axial fire still insisted upon, two of the turrets were winged out and the remaining three placed on the centre-line. The secondary battery was dropped as it was unlikely to be used, but the tertiary battery of anti-torpedo guns was retained. Long-range action also had its problems, especially that of plunging fire; deck armour, therefore, had to be considerably strengthened to resist shell striking at much greater angles. Just as outstanding as the *Dreadnought*'s armament was the decision to install steam turbines for main propulsion; she was the first battleship to be so fitted, and her 3-knot speed advantage over contemporary battleships was achieved with considerable saving in weight and space.

The *Dreadnought* so completely outclassed earlier battleships that her introduction had many important effects. In one stroke the Royal Navy had sacrificed its superiority in

battleships, and had run contrary to its policy of not forcing the pace with increased size. The reason was that similar designs were under active consideration abroad and, rather than follow the prescribed course of 'imitate and overtake', the Royal Navy seized an early start.

The first German and Japanese dreadnought battleships generally followed the British design, and the American ships were also similar but adopted only four centre-line turrets with the inner pair superimposed. Thus, less turrets, they had the same broadside as the others and the loss of direct ahead or astern fire was more theoretical than practical. The classic simplicity of the American arrangement was later universally copied.

The dreadnought cruiser

Having stolen a march with the *Dreadnought*, the Royal Navy did the same with armoured cruisers: vessels ranking second only to battleships in the combatant scale and often surpassing them in size. The armoured cruiser was expanded to accommodate eight 12-inch guns and with the use of turbine machinery secured a conservative 2-knot increase in speed. Like the *Dreadnought*, the *Invincible* completely eclipsed the armoured cruiser, which rapidly became obsolete.

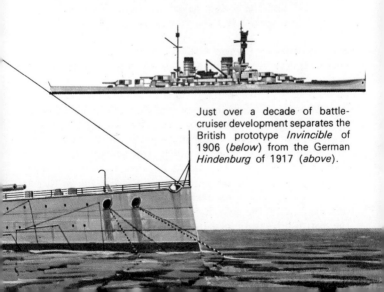

Just over a decade of battle-cruiser development separates the British prototype *Invincible* of 1906 (*below*) from the German *Hindenburg* of 1917 (*above*).

However, putting guns of battleship calibre into a cruiser resulted in its use as a fast wing of the battlefleet, which is not the same thing as duty in the scouting line. The ships came to be called battlecruisers and were retrospectively defined as capital units which sacrificed some of the battleship's armament and protection for speed. However, subsequent battlecruisers conformed with their belated definition and were more realistically armoured. Still beset by the requirement for axial fire, the *Invincible*'s four turrets were disposed one forward, one aft, and one on each beam amidships.

The battlecruiser captured the imagination and enjoyed an enhanced reputation that the First World War was to shatter. The myth was exploded at Jutland when two of the three British losses were attributed to inadequate protection.

There is no denying the tactical advantage gained from high speed, providing it is not secured at too high a price, and five years after the battlecruiser was conceived the Royal Navy, by adopting oil-firing, was able to secure a speed of 25 knots for the 'Queen Elizabeth' class battleships without sacrificing fighting qualities. With the 'Nevada' class battleships the United States Navy reverted to an all-or-nothing system of protection similar to the early turret and barbette ships, and its lead was generally followed by other navies. Thin vertical armour contributed nothing towards protection and was eliminated, and the weight saved was used to augment the thick armour spread over the vital areas.

Battleships between the wars

Following the First World War, battleships were restricted under the terms of the Washington Naval Treaty (1921) to a displacement not exceeding 35,000 tons and guns not larger than 16 inches. Before this, size had increased alarmingly to nearly 50,000 tons to embrace a heavy main armament and thick armour in designs prepared by the American, British, and Japanese navies, none of which came to fruition.

But battleships now had to contend with attack from a third medium: the air. Like the initial torpedo threat, the air threat was at first overrated, but the combination of both in the form of torpedo-carrying aircraft resulted in a serious challenge to the battleship's supremacy. However, while the battleship

Bridge details of the British battlecruiser *Tiger* (1914)

Multiple gun turrets were a feature of ship construction between the World Wars. (*Above*) triple turrets in the Italian battleship *Littorio* (1940). (*Below*) the quadruple turrets of the French battlecruiser *Dunkerque* (1937)

never claimed invulnerability to air or torpedo attack, it was never quite the sitting target claimed by the critics, and these forces had to be marshalled in great strength for success.

Air attack could be countered by anti-aircraft guns, by thicker deck armour, and accompanying fighter aircraft. All were adopted, but as it was not possible to incorporate a flight-deck into capital ship designs, although some interesting proposals were made, aircraft were carried in a special accompanying vessel – the aircraft carrier.

From 1921-35 no capital ships were laid down by treaty signatories except Britain and France, who each built a pair; Germany, not subject to the treaty, also built a pair.

The British ships, the *Nelson* and *Rodney*, were interesting

in that they placed their main armament of 16-inch guns in three triple turrets forward so that protection could be concentrated over the shortest possible length. To meet air attack they were given a 6¼-inch thick deck, while the external anti-torpedo bulge – a successful war-time innovation – was replaced by an internal system of longitudinal bulkheads. The secondary anti-torpedo armament was placed in upper-deck turrets aft, and the tertiary armament now comprised the heavy anti-aircraft guns.

With all the main armament grouped forward, the *Nelson* and *Rodney* were criticized for lack of astern fire, but the merits of the arrangement were not lost on the French Navy when it later built the basically similar, but somewhat smaller, *Dunkerque* and *Strasbourg*. These vessels grouped the main armament forward in two large quadruple turrets, and a dual-purpose secondary armament replaced the separate anti-torpedo and anti-aircraft batteries of the British ships. The French ships were smaller than the British pair, but their speed was stepped up to 29½ knots and they heralded the introduction of the fast battleship.

The two German vessels, the *Gneisenau* and *Scharnhorst*, were more conservative and disposed their main armament forward and aft. Although rated as battlecruisers, they sacrificed no protection to make 32 knots; neither did they sacrifice gunpower. They shipped 11-inch guns as there was no larger calibre available at the time, and the intention was to rearm them later with twin 15-inch replacing the triple

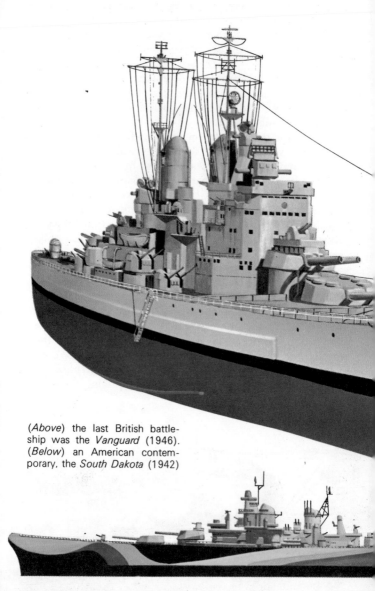

(*Above*) the last British battleship was the *Vanguard* (1946).
(*Below*) an American contemporary, the *South Dakota* (1942)

11-inch turrets. Both secondary and tertiary armaments were shipped and the latter, fourteen heavy guns controlled by four high-angle directors, showed an appreciation of the air threat well in advance of other navies.

The fast battleship

When the Washington Treaty lapsed at the end of 1935 immediate construction began on new capital ships within the specified limits by all signatories except Japan, who refused to be bound by the 35,000-ton, 16-inch gun limit and thereafter drew a veil of secrecy over her activities.

All the new battleships aimed for high speed without sacrificing military qualities and incorporated adequate

vertical and horizontal protection, improved aerial defence, and aircraft for spotting and reconnaissance duties.

The United States Navy unhesitatingly went to the upper limit in gunpower for the *North Carolina* and *Washington* and arranged their nine 16-inch guns in triple turrets forward and aft; the same arrangement was adopted by the Italians for the *Littorio* and *Vittorio Veneto*, but they dropped to 15-inch guns as they wanted more speed; 15-inch guns were also fitted to the French *Richelieu* and *Jean Bart* and the German *Bismarck* and *Tirpitz*, but while the former mounted their eight guns in two quadruple turrets forward, the latter conservatively grouped their guns in twin turrets forward and aft; and the Royal Navy, who were already committed to the 14-inch gun, shipped ten in two quadruple turrets in the *King George V* and *Prince of Wales*, arranging one forward and one aft, with the addition of a twin turret forward.

The succeeding American 'South Dakota' class were similar to the *North Carolina* but were 50 feet shorter, while the 'Iowa' class advanced to 45,000 tons and attained 33 knots, a speed unmatched by any other battleship or battlecruiser for that matter. The projected 'Montana' class had an additional triple 16-inch turret aft.

Two more 'Littorio' class were built by the Italian Navy, but Germany never advanced the projected six 56,200-ton battleships with diesel engines and 16-inch guns.

Two more French vessels of the 'Richelieu' class were never completed, and the final unit was modified with the quadruple turrets distributed forward and aft. Three more 'King George V' class were built by the Royal Navy, but the following 'Lion' class – which were all cancelled – reverted to 16-inch guns disposed as in the *North Carolina*, with a corresponding

The largest battleship ever built was the Japanese *Yamato* (1941), finally sunk by American naval aircraft

rise in displacement to 40,000 tons. One other battleship, the *Vanguard*, was completed to utilize spare 15-inch turrets.

The Japanese giants

As noted earlier, strict secrecy shrouded Japanese naval construction from 1936, so that it was not until after the Second World War that accurate details were available.

Well aware that they would be unable to match American numerical supremacy with capital ships, the Japanese designed the 'Yamato' class as individually superior to any battleship afloat, and as a result the vessels dwarfed contemporary American and European construction. In all, five ships were projected, of which only the first two – the *Yamato* and *Musashi* – were completed as battleships.

With a final standard displacement of 64,170 tons, they were designed to mount nine 18-inch guns in triple turrets, two forward and one aft; eight 8-inch in twin turrets disposed in lozenge fashion; and an anti-aircraft battery of twelve 5-inch in twin turrets and twenty-four 25-millimetre in triple shields. Six aircraft were carried aft with two training catapults at the stern. This armament was later modified.

Protection was on a massive scale with special attention to underwater damage; above the water-line the belt armour was applied externally but below it was behind the hull. The side was invulnerable to 18-inch gunfire at 20,000 yards and the deck to a 2,000-pound bomb dropped from 10,000 feet.

Main propulsion was provided by geared turbines of 150,000 shp, taking steam at 350 lb/in^2 and 800°F from twelve boilers, and driving four shafts for a speed of 27½ knots.

These ships were the ultimate in battleship design and make an interesting comparison with the *Warrior* (see page 8).

SEAPLANE AND AIRCRAFT CARRIERS

The seaplane carrier

Soon after its inception the value of the aircraft for reconnaissance was recognized and, fitted with floats, it was adapted for naval purposes.

To accommodate seaplanes, the earliest mother ship – the British seaplane carrier *Ark Royal* – was converted from a standard commercial collier with machinery arranged aft. The sheer was cut out of the hull, and the holds were used for stowing seaplanes, which were hoisted in and out by travelling steam deck cranes. The seaplanes took off and landed on the water, but as this was very much a smooth-water operation their use was fairly restricted.

By the outbreak of the First World War aircraft had already assumed an offensive role and could carry either bombs or torpedoes, so that in 1914 the Royal Navy acquired and fitted out a number of fast cross-channel steamers as seaplane carriers. They were provided with a hangar and cranes aft, could carry four seaplanes, and were generally armed with four 12-pounder guns. One of them, the *Engadine*, was present at the battle of Jutland.

The limitations of water take-off and landing had been

realized before the war, and both the American and British navies had experimented with aircraft taking off from improvized runways fitted to anchored warships. In 1910 a wheeled aircraft took off from a flight-deck fitted over the fore end of the American cruiser *Birmingham*, and in the

British conversions during the First World War: the seaplane carrier *Engadine* (*above*) and the aircraft carrier *Campania* (*below*)

following year another landed on an after flight-deck on the battleship *Pennsylvania*. In the same year the first British aircraft became airborne from the runway on the fo'c'sle of a battleship, the *Africa*.

The early aircraft carrier

In 1914 the Royal Navy took over the liner *Campania* and fitted her with an inclined flight-deck which ran from bridge to stem. When it was later found necessary to lengthen this deck, the fore funnel was split and the deck passed through it. The *Campania* was the first vessel to use a lift to transfer aircraft from the hangar floor to the flight-deck. The successful outcome of several years' experimental work was an aircraft launched from a catapult fitted on the quarter-deck of the American armoured cruiser *North Carolina* in 1915 while she was under way. The original intention behind the

The British ship *Furious* is portrayed (*below*) after her second conversion to the role of aircraft carrier. The smaller picture is of later date and shows her after a third conversion.

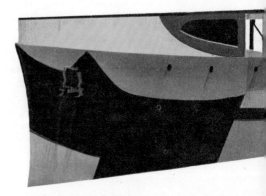

catapult was to launch aircraft from warships not fitted with flying-off decks, but the system was later to play an important part in the evolution of the aircraft carrier.

In 1917 the British cruiser *Furious* was modified when her forward 18-inch turret was removed and replaced with a flying-off deck with hangar space below it. From this deck the first take-off and landing while under way were accomplished, the latter being particularly hazardous. A landing-on deck was provided the following year when the aft 18-inch turret was removed. The cruiser *Cavendish*, which was similarly converted and renamed *Vindictive*, showed the feasibility of this application to a smaller ship.

The separate flying-off and landing-on decks of the *Furious* were a makeshift arrangement dictated by war expediency, and there were obvious disadvantages, such as the transfer outboard of aircraft from the after to the forward deck. But even

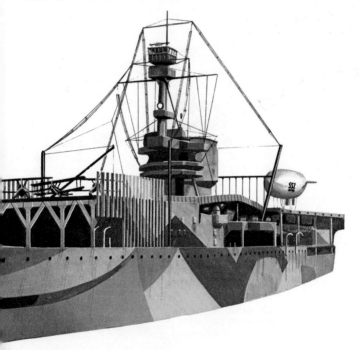

before alterations had been effected the next bold step of providing a completely decked-over vessel had been planned. In selecting suitable ships for conversion the Royal Navy did not have a wide choice, and the incomplete hulls of the Chilean battleship *Almirante Cochrane* (renamed *Eagle*) and the Italian liner *Conte Rosso* (renamed *Argus*) were acquired for this purpose in 1916-7. Also, an order was placed for the first vessel specifically designed as a carrier, the *Hermes,* an example that was soon followed in Japan with the *Hosho.*

The *Argus* was completed first and was a flush-decked vessel with the smoke discharged at the stern through horizontal ducts along the side. For navigational purposes there was a retractable charthouse at the fore end of the flight-deck with small bridge positions on each side. A novel arrangement, however, was adopted by the *Eagle*; the bridge

Sopwith Pup aircraft circling above the British carrier *Argus* which was converted from an Italian liner during the First World War

and funnels were fitted as an island superstructure on the starboard side of the flight-deck. Experience showed that this was a preferable arrangement and it was universally copied. Both vessels had hangars below the flight-deck which were connected by centre-line lifts, but only those of the *Eagle* were double-storeyed.

There was considerable interest in the *Hermes* (10,850 tons) and the *Hosho* (9,494 tons), the first custom-built carriers. They were both much smaller than the *Argus* (14,450 tons) and the *Eagle* (22,600 tons), and yet they were able to stow just as many aircraft. The only American example at this particular time was the flush-decked carrier *Langley* (ex-*Jupiter*) which had been converted from a fleet collier. She carried her aircraft partly dismantled in the holds, from which they were hoisted by cranes to the upper-deck and then transferred by lift to the flight-deck. The *Langley* could, however, stow fifty-five aircraft – this was a considerable increase on the twenty carried by the British vessels – and she was fitted with a catapult because her slow speed was inadequate in light airs.

Conversions from capital ships

As a result of the Washington Naval Treaty there were numerous cancellations in capital ship construction, and many of these hulls were converted to aircraft carriers. Both Japan and the United States retained two battlecruiser hulls for this purpose, and France the hull of a battleship. The terms of the treaty, however, determined that the British cruisers *Courageous* and *Glorious* would have to be included in the total tonnage allocated to capital ships if retained as armed. This was highly undesirable, so they were put in hand for conversion to carriers, together with the *Furious,* which was to undergo a third major alteration. Following the earthquake

disaster of 1923 the Japanese plans were modified as one of the battlecruiser hulls was so damaged that it had to be scrapped and replaced by the hull of a cancelled battleship.

The first of these conversions to pass into service was the British *Furious* in 1925. Although the forward flying-off deck was still retained, a large flight-deck was added at a higher level abaft it and extended unobstructed to the stern. Smoke was discharged aft through horizontal ducts and navigational arrangements similar to those in the *Argus* – a retractable charthouse and wing bridge positions – were adopted. For a time aircraft were operated from two levels, but the use of the forward flying-off deck was later discontinued.

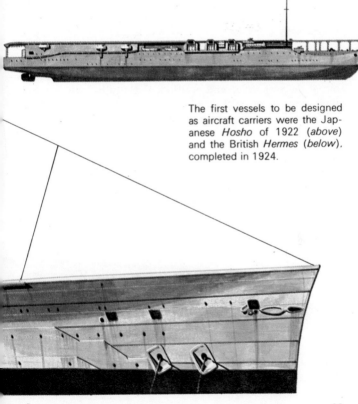

The first vessels to be designed as aircraft carriers were the Japanese *Hosho* of 1922 (*above*) and the British *Hermes* (*below*), completed in 1924.

Two years later the American vessels, the *Lexington* and *Saratoga*, were completed and for many years were the largest examples of their kind. They adopted the island arrangement, had a most conspicuous funnel, and went to treaty limits with armament, mounting eight 8-inch guns in twin turrets forward and aft of the island superstructure. The original battlecruiser turbo-electric machinery was retained and their sustained 33 knots set a standard only recently surpassed.

The French *Béarn* was not outstanding, since the French Navy lacked previous experience in this field, but with a speed of only 21½ knots and a radius of action on the low side the *Béarn* had to operate mainly with the battlefleet.

The first Japanese vessel, the *Akagi*, was flush decked and similar to the British *Furious* except that two flying-off decks – one above and abaft the other – were provided forward, followed by the main flight-deck at a higher level. The funnel arrangement was grotesque: the main exhaust projected horizontally from the starboard side and was turned down at its outboard end, while the auxiliary exhaust was trunked out at the ship's side and positioned vertically with its top at flight-deck level. She was armed with 8-inch guns; there were twin turrets to port and starboard on the lower flying-off

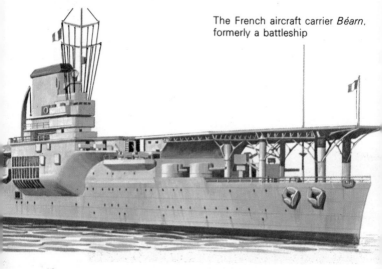

The French aircraft carrier *Béarn*, formerly a battleship

The American aircraft carrier *Lexington*, an ex-battlecruiser, could steam at 33 knots.

deck forward and three guns on each side aft in main-deck casemates. The *Kaga* that followed was generally similar except that smoke was led aft through horizontal ducts running along the side, and she was a little slower as her installed power (intended for a battleship) was lower.

Finally, the British pair, the *Courageous* and *Glorious*, was very similar to the *Furious*, and benefited by experience gained with her. Although the flying-off deck forward was retained, it was never used for this purpose; the island arrangement was adopted for bridge and funnels, and the gun armament was restricted to defensive anti-aircraft guns.

The fleet aircraft carrier

It must be emphasized that the effectiveness of a carrier was firmly linked with the overall efficiency of its air group. Superior ship performance on its own was not enough; it had to be matched – if not exceeded – by aircraft performance, otherwise it was like arming a new battleship with muzzle-loading guns. Here, the Japanese and United States navies were fortunate in retaining control of their own air services, unlike the Royal Navy. This basic difference directly influenced their opposing carrier philosophies. The Royal Navy looked to its carriers to provide air superiority over its own fleet while acting in concert with it; but the United States Navy had evolved the task group concept with its carriers securing air superiority over the enemy fleet while detached from, although acting with, its own fleet. The task group concept was more flexible because it could easily be adapted to other offensive tactics, and the defensive British attitude visualized carriers being detached only for trade protection duties: a problem that was admittedly not as vital to America. The United States Navy, with aircraft development firmly in its own hands, could see ahead, while the Royal Navy was blindfold with the reins in hands other than its own. The Japanese carrier philosophy was also on American lines.

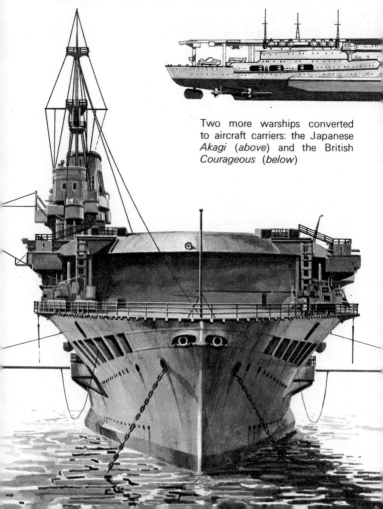

Two more warships converted to aircraft carriers: the Japanese *Akagi* (*above*) and the British *Courageous* (*below*)

Not unnaturally, the experience gained from this varied collection of carriers influenced future designs. Under the terms of the Washington Naval Treaty aircraft carriers were limited in size and total tonnage; they were defined as vessels between 10,000 and 27,000 tons so that below the lesser displacement they did not rank as carriers and were excluded from the total tonnage figure. The Japanese Navy took full advantage of this clause in designing the *Ryujo*, which was laid down in 1929 as an 8,000-ton vessel with a single

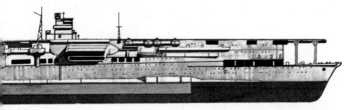

hangar. However, during her construction, the first London Naval Treaty (1930) closed this loophole, and the *Ryujo's* design was modified to improve her combatant value. A second hangar-deck was added to increase aircraft capacity, but this affected her stability and thus resulted in a reduction of the defensive armament. The *Ryujo* was therefore never a wholly satisfactory vessel but she had a novel arrangement for the bridge, which was sited well forward below the fore end of the flight-deck.

In 1931 the United States Navy laid down the medium-sized *Ranger*, in which the main design feature was aircraft capacity, showing a true appreciation of her function. Consequently, the *Ranger* was slower and less well protected than her contemporaries, and although she had an island superstructure the boiler uptakes were led to six hinged funnels well aft which were lowered to a horizontal position during flying operations. The *Yorktown*, laid down four years later, was slightly larger to incorporate all-round improvements. Speed and radius were increased, protection improved, and the machinery placed amidships so that the funnel formed part of the island superstructure.

The *Soryu*, a vessel basically similar to the *Yorktown*, was laid down by the Japanese Navy in the same year and illustrated

Still in service is the British aircraft carrier *Ark Royal* (1946); she is currently being modernized.

the parallel development taking place in both navies. A sister ship, the *Hiryu*, experimented with the island placed on the port side, but as the funnel uptakes were still brought up to starboard this only increased the air disturbance over the flight-deck.

In 1935 the Royal Navy started work on the *Ark Royal*. She proved a worthy contemporary of the American and

The American aircraft carrier *Enterprise* (1938)

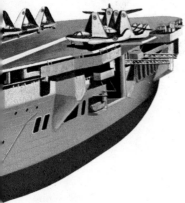

Japanese vessels but was larger, had a heavier defensive armament, and was better protected. The hull plating was extended to the flight-deck, which made her very dry forward, and she was unmatched for seaworthiness.

The *Wasp,* a diminutive of the 'Yorktown' class, was laid down in 1936 by the United States Navy, and was especially interesting. She had athwartship catapults fitted at hangar-deck level, in addition to the more usual fore-and-aft catapults at the fore end of the flight-deck, and a deck-edge lift. The former encroached on, and the latter saved, hangar-deck space, so the one was abandoned and the other retained.

The next year four units of the 'Illustrious' class were laid down by the Royal Navy, and their outstanding feature was that the whole hangar structure – deck, sides, and roof – became an armoured box incorporated with the hull. The

A Fairey Gannet aircraft stowed on the lift of a carrier

penalty was that only a single hangar could be provided and the aircraft capacity (compared with *Ark Royal*) was halved, but it ensured their survival in areas where carriers were exposed to heavy air attack. Later, the aircraft capacity was increased by accepting deck-stowed planes and by incorporating a half-hangar in the last unit. Two further vessels were very similar and incorporated the half-hangar from the outset, but the side armour was much reduced in thickness.

Two Japanese carriers laid down in the same year were expansions of the *Soryu* design, now that all treaty limitations had lapsed, and with the 'Essex' class – started in 1941 – the United States Navy advanced to dimensions approaching those of the battlecruiser conversions. Although aircraft capacity remained on a par with earlier carriers they were all able to operate larger and heavier aircraft, but with more tonnage devoted to ship performance.

Japan, however, had undertaken some construction in this category which had not been detected. Several years earlier the Japanese Imperial Navy planned a series of fast auxiliary vessels suitable for conversion to carriers, and this programme was secretly completed. Two submarine depot ships and one mercantile liner conversion were placed in service during 1941 and were joined, in the following year, by conversions from another depot ship and four more liners. Therefore, over a very short period the Imperial Navy was able to double its carrier strength, and while the conversions did not match the more recent fleet vessels, the availability of sixteen carriers in 1942 proved decisive at a vital moment.

Before the outbreak of the Second World War the only other navies to embark on carrier construction were France and Germany. The French vessels had the flight-decks offset to port, and, while dimensionally similar to the *Yorktown* and *Soryu*, they had only half their aircraft capacity. German carrier construction was hampered at every turn by inexperience and the German Air Force's complete lack of co-operation. Designed to operate with the raiding capital ship squadrons, much of the vessels' tonnage was devoted to ship features with a corresponding reduction in aircraft capacity. They shipped a heavy armament of low-angle and high-angle guns, and were fast with an adequate radius of action. None of these vessels was ever completed, and only the German *Graf Zeppelin* reached the launching stage.

The escort aircraft carrier

When exposed to the stern test of war the carrier soon asserted itself, and was wielded with telling effect by the Royal Navy at Taranto, the Imperial Navy at Pearl Harbor, and the United States Navy at Midway. In the Pacific as early as 1942 the carrier became the capital unit around which a task group was formed, but even earlier than that it had shown itself equally vital in the Atlantic convoy battle.

Outside the range of shore-based maritime aircraft on both sides of the Atlantic was a wide area in which convoys were deprived of air cover unless a carrier was available. Fleet carriers were too few and valuable to be exposed to this duty,

American escort carriers: a 'Prince William' class unit (*above*) and the *Long Island* of 1941 (*below*)

and a less sophisticated carrier was adequate. From this concept was evolved the escort aircraft carrier which need carry only a small number of aircraft at moderate speed.

The earliest example was the British *Audacity*, which was converted from a German mercantile prize in 1940. Her superstructure was cut down, and a flight-deck added; she carried six deck-stowed aircraft at 15 knots, and she enjoyed a short-lived but conclusive success. Under the terms of 'Lease/Lend' the United States soon after put in hand ten conversions (shared equally between the United States and Royal navies). With the later American entry into the war, production was stepped up significantly, and no less than 129 orders (113 completed and 16 subsequently cancelled) had been placed by the end of hostilities. With the 'Casablanca' class building time was progressively cut from eight to three and a half months; it took only one year and a day for the whole class of fifty-five units to be commissioned.

In comparison the Japanese output was small and only four further conversions were effected – two from mercantile liners and two from naval seaplane carriers – but as they were for front-line duty their conversions were much more elaborate. Both the Italian and German navies proposed mercantile conversions during the war but none ever came to fruition, although the Italian *Aquila* was well advanced and was protected by a concrete bulge $23\frac{1}{2}$ inches thick.

The merchant aircraft carrier

Until the American escort carrier programme was in full swing a British project was introduced as an interim measure: the merchant aircraft carrier (MAC). The conversion could be undertaken only with bulk carriers which could dispense

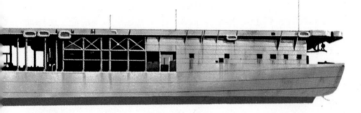

with the normal cargo hatches; six grain carriers and four tankers were altered during construction and nine other tankers (two under the Dutch flag) were converted. The original Admiralty specification had called for a speed of 14 or 15 knots and a flight-deck measuring 490 × 62 feet, but this was reduced to 11 knots and 390 × 62 feet so that standard war cargo hulls could be used. The grain carriers were provided with a hangar and lift, which could be omitted from the longer tankers whose after flight-decks served as a permanent deck park for aircraft. Both types shipped four aircraft and a naval air complement, but were otherwise mercantile manned. With a fair measure of success they were used both as merchant ship and aircraft carrier during a critical period. A somewhat similar plan was adopted in Japan towards the close of the war with five tankers under construction. But such was the shortage of oil fuel that she had to revert to coal-firing cargo vessels, which prevented them from being decked-over to operate aircraft.

War construction

The construction of fleet aircraft carriers was naturally much intensified after the outbreak of the Second World War.

With many other equally important commitments the Royal Navy could not undertake any large-scale programme, especially as it was completely dependent on the United States for naval aircraft. Therefore only four slightly enlarged 'Illustrious' class were projected with full double hangars and armour, followed by three 45,000-ton units. Only two of the former were laid down and the rest were cancelled.

The United States, on the other hand, was absolutely dependent on carriers for the Pacific war, and the 'Essex' class – which proved most successful – were expanded to thirty-two units, while the succeeding 'Midway' class advanced to 45,000 tons and were armoured on the British principle. The end of hostilities eventually resulted in eight of the former and three of the latter being cancelled.

Carriers were equally essential to Japan, but shortages in most of the essential materials had a crippling effect on

production. Ambitious programmes were proposed but they remained paper projects with no hope of fulfilment.

The *Taiho*, laid down shortly before the Japanese entry into the war, finally emerged as the only unit of her type, although two more – later four – were planned. The main features of the *Taiho* – a single armoured hangar and a strong defensive armament – bore a close resemblance to those of the British *Illustrious*. Unlike the usual horizontal arrangement, the funnel was stepped vertically but it was nevertheless inclined outboard at a bizarre angle.

Another war completion was the *Shinano*, which had been laid down as a battleship of the 'Yamato' class and was converted to a carrier while being built. Despite her bulk – she greatly surpassed even the 45,000-ton American 'Midway' class – the *Shinano*'s aircraft capacity was small, mainly due to the acute shortage of planes and pilots. She was, however, amply provided with facilities for refuelling aircraft from other carriers, but the intention to use her as a support platform was frustrated by her premature loss.

The design of the 'Unryu' class, which reverted to the smaller dimensions and general arrangement of the *Hiryu*, was more realistic but of the seventeen vessels planned the last eleven were not even laid down. In fact, the 'Unryu' class

The British *Eagle* (1924) was the first aircraft carrier to adopt an island superstructure — offset to starboard — a practice that later was universally adopted.

reflected the Japanese solution to a problem which had earlier beset the United States Navy: that the construction and trials of a fleet carrier took such a long time. In the critical years of 1942-3 the United States Navy could not afford to wait on long-term construction, and this resulted in a crash programme of light fleet carriers.

The light fleet carrier

The most suitable hulls available for rapid conversion were those of the 'Cleveland' class light cruisers, and nine – all constructed in one yard – were selected for this purpose. The original machinery remained unaltered but deep bulges were added to the hull to improve stability, and with four short funnels (arranged in pairs) they were certainly distinctive. Although they were restricted both in capacity and the type of aircraft that could be stowed, they nevertheless proved effective stopgaps and two slightly enlarged units were later put in hand.

Similar conversions were undertaken with the cruisers *Seydlitz* and *Ibuki* by Germany and Japan but they were uncompleted by the end of the war.

For general fleet duties the light fleet carrier also appealed to the Royal Navy but with the essential difference that it would have to be specially built. In 1939 the aircraft maintenance carrier *Unicorn*, which was designed to service shipborne aircraft, had been laid down. While she was decked for landing and flying-off purposes, she carried no aircraft of her own but was provided below decks with workshops and stores for her support task. Although the *Unicorn* would have proved most useful in her designed role, she was nevertheless completed as an operational carrier and served as a model for the subsequent light fleet carriers. To reduce building time their hulls were constructed to the requirements of Lloyd's Register, and simple, rugged and

austere standards were adopted throughout. Two very similar classes totalling sixteen vessels were ordered, of which two were completed as maintenance carriers and one other was never completed. Whatever their shortcomings, seven are still in service today with the navies of Argentina, Australia, Brazil, Canada, France, India and the Netherlands; it was the most internationally popular class of major warship.

The aircraft carrier in the atomic age

With the advent of the atomic bomb the survival of the aircraft carrier – like all major surface warships – was put in jeopardy, because so obvious a target as a carrier task group would invite attack. The problems associated with the group's air defence were not insuperable, and passive measures that could easily be implemented were greater dispersal, earlier detection and improved interception of targets. By the late 1940s, therefore, although the resilient carrier was considered not indestructible, she was difficult to detect and hard to destroy. Nor should it be forgotten that carrier aircraft could also deliver atomic bombs, and the ability to strike back in kind was in itself a deterrent.

A Hurricane aircraft being catapulted from a specially fitted British merchant ship during the Second World War

Three notable British advances have considerably improved flight-deck operations: the angled deck, the mirror landing aid, and the steam catapult. By these means it is possible to launch and recover aircraft simultaneously, accommodate higher landing speeds safely, and launch the much heavier aircraft now in operation. The United States added deck-edge lifts and deck parks so that the flight-deck, formerly a fairly regular rectangle, now assumed an irregular shape. With the island superstructure still to starboard, the angled deck is run off to port. Four deck-edge lifts are fitted amidships, three to starboard and one to port, and four catapults are provided, two each at the forward ends of the angled deck and flight-deck.

The type of aircraft operated determines the size of the flight-deck, and with the 800 feet required by modern aircraft the carrier has continued to advance in size. Not

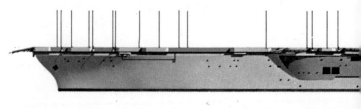

Profile and aerial view of the American nuclear-powered aircraft carrier *Enterprise* (1961)

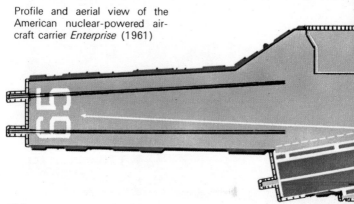

surprisingly displacement has risen from 59,600 tons with the American *Forrestal* – the first postwar-designed carrier – to the 75,700 tons of the *Enterprise*, currently the largest carrier afloat. The latter is nuclear powered; she is propelled by four sets of geared steam turbines totalling 360,000 shp at a speed of 36 knots, and tactically has an unlimited high-speed endurance. For defensive purposes the *Enterprise* primarily relies on her own aircraft together with the weapons of her accompanying escorts, but as a final self-defence capability against aircraft she ships two guided missile systems. Her high speed is her best defence against submarines, and she can be completely replenished at sea by a fleet of fast support ships. Until manned aircraft are completely supplanted by missiles there appears little likelihood of the carrier being made obsolete, and she has amply demonstrated her ability over the past twenty years.

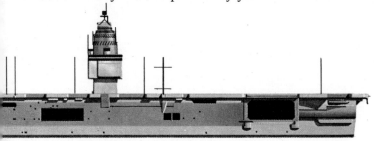

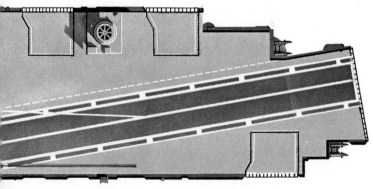

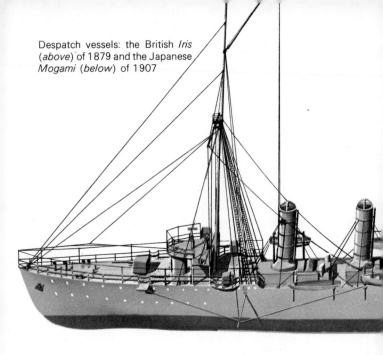

Despatch vessels: the British *Iris* (*above*) of 1879 and the Japanese *Mogami* (*below*) of 1907

CRUISERS

The iron frigate and corvette

The main functions of the cruiser were to scout for the battle-fleet, to protect trade, and – before the introduction of wireless telegraphy – to repeat signals and carry urgent despatches. For all these duties the cruiser required speed together with a good radius of action. Therefore, the general adoption of steam propulsion was of more importance to the cruiser than the use of iron for construction. The latter did, however, mean that the hull could be longer and lighter, and this was not forgotten in the desire to secure high speed.

Cruiser requirements varied so considerably between different navies that any generalization is difficult. Development is best studied among the maritime nations which had overseas possessions and were therefore dependent on maintaining communications and protecting trade; the navies of such countries required cruisers of all types.

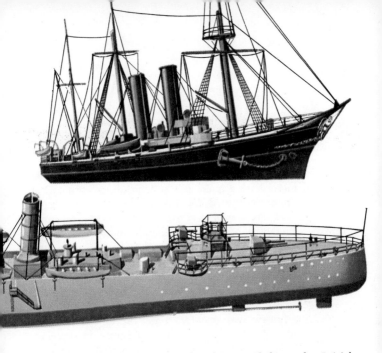

The earliest iron frigates were large and fast – the British *Inconstant* was of 5,780 tons and steamed at 16 knots – and they were, of course, fully rigged. As they were too costly to build in large numbers an almost immediate reaction was to adopt a smaller iron corvette of slightly less speed. In both cases the armament was still carried on the broadside with manually-operated light chase guns at the bow and stern.

Smaller than the corvette, and with a good turn of speed, was the despatch vessel. It was very lightly armed as its machinery absorbed a large proportion of the available weight and space. As early as 1879 the British *Iris* was steaming at 18 knots and, at the time, was the world's fastest warship.

The submerged armoured deck

As cruisers on distant stations could be confronted by small armoured vessels with which they would be unable to close for decisive action, the cruising ironclad made its first appearance. The prototype British vessel – the *Shannon* – was designed to

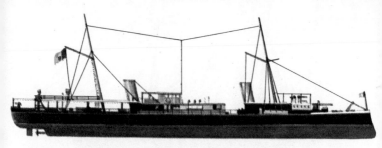

fight end-on, in which position she presented a deep armoured bulkhead pierced for a main gun at each upper corner; but she is better remembered for introducing the submerged armoured deck. As ranges were still short, and the trajectory correspondingly flat, only thin horizontal armour was required for a substantial degree of protection. Until this time little thought had been given to the protection of cruising vessels owing to the weight involved, but as the armoured deck enabled even a small weight allowance to be usefully spread it was generally adopted.

Once the full rig was abandoned and breech-loading guns were introduced, there was marked progress in development. A fully-rigged corvette, with a partially-armoured deck over the machinery spaces, that could make 13 knots was, within a few years, matched by a twin-screw vessel with a complete armoured deck able to steam at 16 knots. Although the sides of the armoured deck still remained below the water-line, the crown was arched to slightly above the water-line so that there was more headroom in the boiler and engine rooms. This countered the objection that with the side pierced sufficient water could collect over the flat

Torpedo cruisers: the Italian *Partenope* of 1890 (*above*) and the British *Scout* (*below*), completed in 1885

armoured deck to affect stability, because with the crown arched water was now restricted to the narrow channels on each side.

The general arrangement of cruising vessels largely followed traditional practice with a fo'c'sle and poop joined by a high bulwark behind which guns were carried on the broadside. Cruisers retained the broadside system longer than battleships as it better suited their type of action. They would generally make the first contact with the enemy on the fringes of their respective fleets and, in the ensuing *mêlée*, it was more than likely that they would be engaged with enemy vessels on both sides.

The Elswick cruiser

Armstrongs established their reputation for cruisers in 1885 when they completed the *Esmeralda* for Chile. Fo'c'sle, poop, and bulwark went by the board; heavy 10-inch, 25-ton chase guns were positioned fore and aft and the medium 6-inch, 4-ton guns amidships; protection was afforded by a complete armoured deck; and a speed of over 18 knots was realized. All this was achieved on a displacement of under 3,000 tons, and for the next twenty years the Elswick cruiser was to be

a pace-setter synonymous with heavy armament and high speed on a small displacement.

The torpedo cruiser

The torpedo cruiser was conceived as an ocean-going torpedo boat: a sound idea, somewhat ahead of its time. The speed and frailty of the torpedo boat were sacrificed for a larger and more seaworthy hull, and the vessel carried about ten fixed torpedo tubes in the bow and stern and on the broadside, with only a light gun armament on the fo'c'sle and poop. As it was rather heavily loaded for its 1,500-ton displacement the torpedo cruiser soon lost speed in a seaway and could seldom close to

effective torpedo range except in fine weather. There is little use for a cruiser that cannot operate in good and bad weather; as a type it appeared only briefly on the cruiser scene, and a main armament of torpedoes did not fit it for general service.

The armoured cruiser

Before the turn of the century the construction of any foreign cruiser that could be used against trade usually resulted in an immediate counter by the Royal Navy owing to the absolute dependence of the British Empire on sea communications.

Armoured cruisers: the American *West Virginia* of 1911 (*above*) and the Greek *Averoff* of 1905 (*below*) as she appeared – little altered – in the Second World War

These cruisers (usually termed corsairs) were invariably large vessels with a wide radius of action, high speed, and an armament that included a small number of heavy guns. The Royal Navy found the introduction of corsairs very harrassing, and on more than one occasion was compelled to retaliate by building large cruisers which were otherwise unsuitable for general fleet purposes.

The first British armoured cruisers (the 'Orlando' class) were in many ways a smaller edition of the 'Admiral' class battleships, and were intended to provide protection against corsairs on the trade routes. They were protected by a partial 10-inch belt amidships closed by 16-inch bulkheads, and had a flat 2-inch deck over the belt and an arched 2-inch or 3-inch deck outside the belt extending to the ends. With a 12-inch conning tower and 4-inch gunshields they were protected on a scale that enabled them to engage small armoured tonnage, and were armed with centre-line 9·2-inch guns fore and aft and ten 6-inch guns on the broadside amidships. Their most interesting feature was the provision, for the first time, of triple expansion engines, still fitted horizontally to keep them below the water-line, which gave an additional 1,000 ihp over the compound engines originally proposed and raised the speed by a knot to 19 knots.

The classification of cruisers
The protection afforded by armour led to the armoured or deck protected cruisers being rated above the generally unarmoured cruisers, and while the former were always of the largest size the latter were sub-divided into 1st, 2nd, or 3rd class depending on their tonnage. Where applicable these classifications were applied retrospectively. Cruising ironclads, when not of capital rank, became armoured cruisers, and iron frigates became 1st class protected, corvettes 2nd class protected, and sloops, despatch vessels, and torpedo cruisers 3rd class protected cruisers.

There was a sharp clash of opinion about the application of armour vertically and externally or horizontally and internally, and the seaman's natural aversion to the second method, which allowed shell to penetrate the hull before encountering resistance, was understandable. However, the armoured deck

Two 2nd class protected cruisers: the Italian *Etna* of 1887 (*above*) and the British vessel *Leander* (*below*), completed in 1885

provided equivalent protection at a lower total weight than side armour, and for a fast vessel like a cruiser this was a most attractive feature. In size and performance there was little to choose between an armoured and 1st class protected cruiser.

The protected cruiser

Thus, only two years after the *Orlando* was laid down, the Royal Navy started work on the *Blake*, which had a maximum speed of 22 knots and a large radius so that she could surpass all regular, or auxiliary, cruisers used against trade. Although the armament was the same as the *Orlando*'s, there was a considerable increase in size to accommodate the more powerful machinery and enlarged bunker, and the *Blake* had the first vertical triple expansion engines to be installed in a cruiser. She was protected by a complete arched deck, 3 inches thick on the flat and 6 inches thick on the slopes, and as the cylinder tops of the engines projected above the deck, the deck was gently sloped to enclose and protect them in an armoured *glacis*. At this time the first quick-firing guns were coming

into service, and this may have influenced the departure from side armour; but, while the total weight of armour for the much larger *Blake* was 1,190 tons, the smaller *Orlando* absorbed 960 tons, and the figures speak for themselves.

Most 2nd and 3rd class protected cruisers retained the arrangement of a short fo'c'sle and poop, on which the chase guns were mounted, with the remaining guns in the waist on each side. Usually the 2nd class vessel had 6-inch chase guns and 6-inch or 4·7-inch guns in the waist, whereas the 3rd class vessel had a uniform battery of 4·7-inch or 4-inch guns. Maximum speeds were about 20 knots in 2nd class vessels and 18 knots in 3rd class vessels.

Cruiser design remained much the same, with no marked increase in speed, until the advent of the British battleship *Dreadnought* forced the issue. Each succeeding class of cruiser incorporated only minor improvements in armament, protection, and machinery, but there were lively disputes over the introduction of forced draught and watertube boilers.

The destruction and protection of commerce

Noteworthy cruisers were the French *Dupuy de Lôme* (1890), the American *Columbia* (1892), and the Russian *Rurik* (1894): all corsairs which the Royal Navy regarded with a baleful eye. The *Dupuy de Lôme* was of 6,300 tons, carried all her main and secondary guns in turrets, and was protected by 4-inch armour along the entire hull to the upper-deck. The main

The British 3rd class protected cruiser *Pelorus* (1897)

190-millimetre, 7·5-inch guns were placed on each side amidships and sponsored out for full 180 degree arcs on their respective sides; the secondary 160-millimetre, 6·2-inch guns were arranged three at each end with wide arcs across the bow and stern. With a speed of 20 knots, some two or three knots below foreign contemporaries, the *Dupuy de Lôme* was more prepared to fight it out than avoid action.

The 7,475-ton *Columbia*, on the other hand, was prepared to use her high speed of 22 knots to avoid action rather than her light armament of one 8-inch, two 6-inch, and eight 4-inch guns, although both her speed and armament were adequate for overhauling and sinking even the fastest merchant vessels by gunfire. The slowest of the trio, the *Rurik* could make 18 knots and surprisingly was fully rigged. With a displacement of 10,923 tons she fairly bristled with guns and, if brought to action, could bring four 8-inch, sixteen 6-inch, and six 4·7-inch guns to bear. While the *Columbia* was deck protected, the *Rurik* was protected by a narrow water-line belt, and in both of them all the gun positions were unarmoured.

The *Rurik* prompted the construction of the British *Powerful* and *Terrible*, whose dimensions – 14,200 tons and 538 feet – surpassed even contemporary battleships. They easily made 22 knots but needed forty-eight Belleville boilers to supply

The French armoured cruiser *Dupuy de Lôme* (1895)

the steam. These boilers were of the watertube type and started a bitter dispute about the merits of this and the older cylindrical type. As a result there was a series of competitive tests between cruisers with watertube and cylindrical boilers; the most interesting outcome was the discovery that radius was not limited by bunker capacity but by the amount of reserve feed water carried to make up water losses in the boilers. In the end the watertube boiler showed its superiority and was used in all high-powered warships.

Towards the close of the century there was an unexplained revival in armoured cruiser construction. They were such large and costly vessels that consideration was even given to incorporating them in the line-of-battle, almost – it would appear – to justify their existence. But whatever the reason, they were built by most major navies and were acquired by a few minor navies. The Italian design found much favour abroad, and four were purchased by Argentina, one by Spain, and two by Japan. Such was the run that the name *Giuseppe Garibaldi* was given to four vessels before it finally appeared in the Italian fleet, as the first three were all sold prior to completion! The armoured cruiser was made obsolete by the battlecruiser which, armed with guns of battleship calibre, was finally drawn into the battleline.

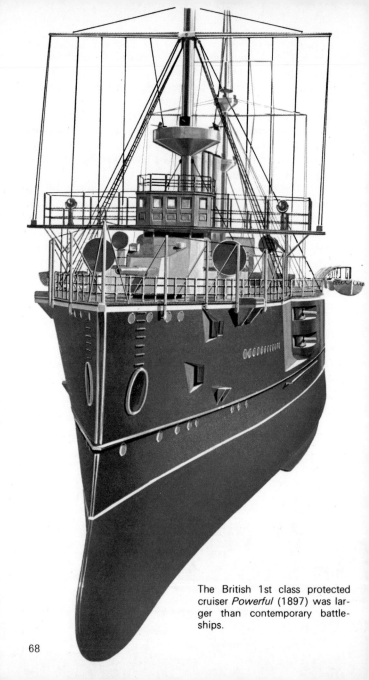

The British 1st class protected cruiser *Powerful* (1897) was larger than contemporary battleships.

The light cruiser

When the battleship *Dreadnought* increased the speed of the battlefleet by some three knots there had to be a similar rise in the speed of fleet cruisers. Fortunately the turbine, which enabled the *Dreadnought* to achieve this increase, was also available to the cruiser, and it led to such a rapid all-round development in design that there was a clear line of demarcation between the turbine cruiser and its earlier reciprocating-engined counterpart.

With armoured and 1st class protected cruisers obsolete, development stemmed from the 2nd and 3rd class cruisers. Thus, on about 5,000 tons displacement, the 2nd class turbine cruiser made 25 knots, adhered to deck protection, carried about ten or twelve guns (either of uniform 4-inch calibre or with heavier 6-inch bow and stern chase pieces), and was suitable for work with the fleet or on the trade routes. The 3rd class turbine cruisers were similar except that they averaged about 3,500 tons, had up to ten 4-inch guns, and were used either as scouts or as leaders for the destroyer flotillas.

The introduction of oil fuel started fresh development at about 3,500 tons, but with an armament comparable to the 2nd class cruiser and with speed increased to 30 knots. However, the cruiser now lost the considerable protection of its coal, which had been arranged over and at the ends and sides of the machinery spaces. To compensate for this loss, thin side armour was again used together with a partially-armoured deck. These vessels were first classed as light armoured cruisers to distinguish them from the old type of armoured cruiser, and later simply as light cruisers, to include the earlier turbine cruisers.

The combination of turbines and oil fuel marked a significant stage in cruiser design and resulted in fast and well-armed vessels of moderate size. They came through the ensuing First World War with an enhanced reputation that was worthily earned in action. The height of their development is best exemplified by the British 'Ceres' class which on 4,200 tons could steam at 29 knots, were sheathed in 2 to 3 inches of armour, and armed with five 6-inch guns all mounted on the centre-line – two forward, one amidships, and two aft – and with the inboard end guns superimposed.

The British *Amethyst* (*below*) brought turbine propulsion to 3rd class protected cruisers. (*Above*) the Austro-Hungarian *Novarra* (1914)

The 'C' class were slightly surpassed in size by the 'D' class of 4,650 tons, but in addition there were two classes constructed to special war requirements:* the 'E' class, which had risen to 7,550 tons to attain 33 knots, and the 'Raleigh' class, which were enlarged to 9,750 tons to mount 7·5-inch guns.

The Washington cruiser

In framing the Washington Naval Treaty the upper limit placed on cruisers was 10,000 tons and 8-inch guns, specifically because of the British 'Raleigh' class as no other navy had a cruiser exceeding 7,000 tons. The unfortunate result of this was not apparent to the Royal Navy until the first series of ships – all built to the limit – were in service, when they were found to be too large and costly for British requirements. However the 10,000-ton treaty cruiser appealed to Japan and the United States and, with France and Italy neutral, there was little sympathy for the British case to restrict cruisers in size and armament still further.

* These requirements were based on war intelligence that the Germans were building fast cruisers and that they intended to fit heavy guns to their mercantile raiders. This information proved false but by that time the ships were so well advanced that only one unit (an 'E' class) could be cancelled.

With the first series of treaty cruisers the French and Italian navies secured high speed by sacrificing protection; the Japanese Navy was content with less speed but gave its ships an additional twin 8-inch turret – making ten 8-inch guns – and better protection (and also exceeded the treaty limit by about 1,000 tons); whereas the British ships were slower than the French and Italian vessels but with no compensation in protection or armament. The Americans were last in the field and they also put ten guns into their ships, like the Japanese, but mounted them in two triple and two twin turrets, and

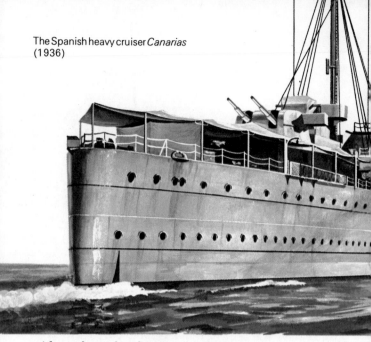

The Spanish heavy cruiser *Canarias* (1936)

with good speed and protection they turned out nearly 1,000 tons under the limit imposed on cruisers by the treaty.

In the second series of treaty cruisers, enhanced protection, at the cost of speed, was incorporated by France and Italy (the latter also going over the limit); improvements were only marginal in Japan and Great Britain; and the United States

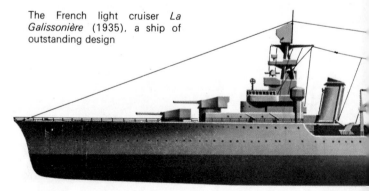

The French light cruiser *La Galissonière* (1935), a ship of outstanding design

created a new design around three triple 8-inch gun turrets.

Substantial protection without loss of speed was the feature of the third series. France and Italy produced singular examples, the United States equally good vessels, and Spain two vessels which were built to a British design. The first breakaway from the 10,000-ton type was by the Royal Navy, which

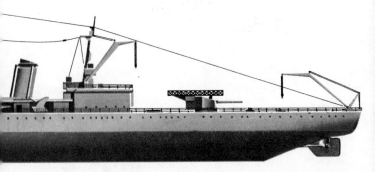

built two diminutives by sacrificing a twin 8-inch turret aft; two similar vessels were built for Argentina in Italy. All the treaty cruisers used side and deck armour except the British vessels of the first and second series which were deck protected. The French *Algérie* was the best example of the treaty type, and although over twenty-five per cent of her weight was devoted to protection she could steam at 31 knots, had a good radius of action, and a strong anti-aircraft battery.

The London cruiser

The first London Naval Treaty brought a halt to the construction of 8-inch gun, 10,000-ton cruisers, and they were now limited in total tonnage so that each navy could interpret its requirements as it chose. Construction now turned to smaller types of vessel armed with 6-inch guns, and they proved very effective. They were generally not extreme examples of any particular feature but a well-balanced compromise including some of the best examples of naval architecture.

The European navies all favoured ships of about 7,000 tons, armed with eight or nine 6-inch guns, but Japan and the United States – who had always favoured the large cruiser – forced the pace. Basically, what Japan did was to modify the heavy cruiser design by replacing twin 8-inch turrets with triple 6-inch turrets, and thus the 'Mogami' class had fifteen guns: nearly double the broadside of contemporary European ships. The Royal Navy felt compelled to counter with the 'Southampton' class (9,100 tons and twelve 6-inch guns), and the United States Navy followed suit with the 'Brooklyn' class (10,000 tons and fifteen 6-inch guns).

The German armoured cruiser

In 1933 the German Navy completed the armoured ship *Deutschland*. She complied with the Treaty of Versailles (1919) in that she was ostensibly a 10,000-ton (actually 11,700-ton) ship armed with 11-inch guns, but although she utilized replacement battleship tonnage she was, in fact, an armoured

Aircraft arrangements on the French heavy cruiser *Algérie* (1934) comprised two training catapults for launching seaplanes; recovery was made by crane.

cruiser. Armed with six 11-inch and eight 5·9-inch guns and with novel diesel propulsion for a speed of 26 knots, it was claimed that the *Deutschland* could outfight any ship she could not outrun, and with the exception of a handful of elderly British and Japanese battlecruisers it was a valid claim. The *Deutschland* so completely outclassed the 8-inch gun cruisers that her appearance helped to stop their construction, except in the United States which lagged behind Europe in implementing her construction programme. Then came the Anglo-German Naval Treaty (1935) under which Germany could build five 8-inch gun cruisers and she benefited by the much publicized shortcomings of the earlier vessels. As the German ships exceeded the tonnage limit by about 3,000 tons they were not surprisingly superior all-round and had exceptionally high steam conditions – over 1,000 lb/in^2.

The flotilla and anti-aircraft cruiser
Despite the upward trend in cruiser construction the value of the small cruiser was always recognized, providing it could incorporate a useful armament on a small displacement. The

The fast and powerful Japanese flotilla cruiser *Yubari* (1923)

The Dutch flotilla cruiser *Tromp* (1938)

lengths to which this could be taken were shown in the Japanese *Yubari* which, on a displacement of 2,890 tons, had the same broadside as the earlier Japanese 5,000-ton light cruisers. The Dutch *Tromp* was an outstanding example of a cruiser designed to work in support of destroyer flotillas. On 3,787 tons she had a speed of 34 knots, was armoured, and mounted six 5·9-inch guns and six 21-inch torpedo tubes.

In 1931 the Royal Navy had converted two old 'C' class vessels to anti-aircraft ships by replacing their 6-inch guns with ten 4-inch guns, and they were favourably received. Surprisingly, in view of their dislike of small cruisers, this development was taken a stage further by the United States Navy with its 'Atlanta' class, which shipped sixteen 5-inch guns in twin turrets. Although the British 'Dido' class are often included in this category they were not specifically

Anti-aircraft cruisers: (*above*) the American *San Juan* and (*below*) the French *De Grasse* (1955), now altered as a command ship

anti-aircraft cruisers, as their dual-purpose main armament of ten 5·25-inch guns was designed as much for use against surface targets as air targets.

War construction

During the Second World War cruisers were used a great deal: there was hardly a major operation in which they were not involved. They were a high priority in those navies which were dependent on sea communications, and Japan's failure to build them proved to be a great mistake. Only the United States embarked on large-scale new construction; most other navies did little more than complete the cruisers they had laid down, or authorized, before the war.

On the whole, the United States Navy built just two types of cruiser at this time: the heavy cruiser with nine 8-inch guns and the light cruiser with twelve 6-inch guns (both had a secondary battery of twelve 5-inch dual-purpose guns). The former ranged from the 13,600-ton 'Baltimore' class to the 17,000-ton 'Des Moines' class, and the latter comprised the

'Cleveland' and 'Fargo' classes of 10,000 tons. In addition there were the 6,000-ton 'Oakland' class, modifications of the *Atlanta*, which were enlarged to the 14,700-ton 'Worcester' class with twelve 6-inch dual-purpose guns in fully automatic twin turrets; and the large 27,500-ton 'Alaska' class with a main armament of nine 12-inch guns.

After the war there was a period of reappraisal owing to the atom bomb, and the gun-armed cruiser became obsolete as, with 16-inch gun battleships supplanted, there was even less need for vessels armed with 8-inch and 6-inch guns. But at least the cruiser passed out of service gracefully: there were no wholesale scrappings, although at the end of their effective lives they were dismantled. The most surprising feature of the postwar years was the large programme of cruisers put in hand by the Soviet Union. Of 15,450 tons, the Russian vessels were fast, well protected, and armed with twelve 5·9-inch and twelve 3·9-inch guns.

Many hulls left incomplete during, and after, the war years were completed to fresh and interesting designs. The French

De Grasse finally emerged as an anti-aircraft cruiser and shipped sixteen 5-inch and sixteen 57-millimetre guns in twin turrets at five different levels. Dual-purpose major and secondary guns were the feature of the Dutch and British vessels; the former received eight 6-inch and eight 57-millimetre guns and the latter four 6-inch and six 3-inch guns, all in twin power-

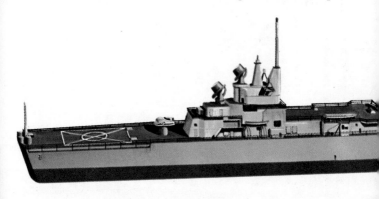

operated turrets. The United States converted most of her cruisers to carry guided missiles and with their large array of radar aerials they have lost their attractive appearance.

The guided missile cruiser
There are few cruiser characteristics in the current guided missile cruiser. The name is more one of convenience as the vessels are too large to be satisfactorily classed with frigates and destroyers. The sole American example, the *Long Beach*, is outstanding in that she is nuclear powered and displaces 14,200 tons. The Italian and Russian vessels of this type are expanded frigate designs, approaching 6,000 tons, built to provide air and anti-submarine defence, but the most recent Italian example – the *Vittorio Veneto* – is of 8,000 tons and incorporates four Polaris missiles in addition to her defensive capability.

A small number of gun-armed cruisers are still retained to lend gunfire support to troops ashore, but it is unlikely that they will be replaced when their service is ended. The cruiser's scouting duties are now undertaken by aircraft and radar,

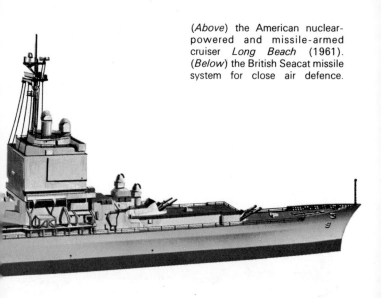

(*Above*) the American nuclear-powered and missile-armed cruiser *Long Beach* (1961). (*Below*) the British Seacat missile system for close air defence.

her main guns have been outranged by aircraft and missiles, and her trade protection duties are carried out by the frigate. The term cruiser, like destroyer, now merely indicates an approximation of size, and it will probably continue to be applied to large frigates.

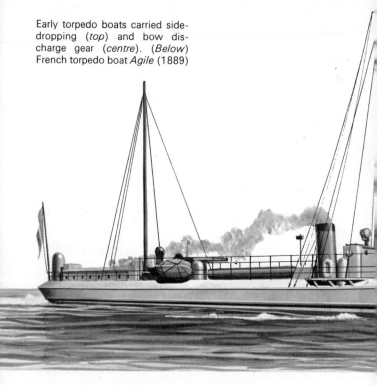

Early torpedo boats carried side-dropping (*top*) and bow discharge gear (*centre*). (*Below*) French torpedo boat *Agile* (1889)

TORPEDO BOATS AND DESTROYERS

Torpedo boats and launches

The torpedo had always had the advantage that it could be carried by a small craft. As it was automotive its discharge was a relatively simple matter, yet its power was sufficient to sink, or seriously damage, the largest vessel.

The earliest torpedo boats (about 1875) were as fast as existing machinery permitted, and mechanical limitations restricted dimensions to secure high speed. Torpedoes were carried on each side in dropping gear, which was turned out when required for action, rather like boats under davits. In consequence, it was necessary to aim the boat at the target, and this principle was maintained, despite later advances with torpedoes and control equipment, until fairly recent times.

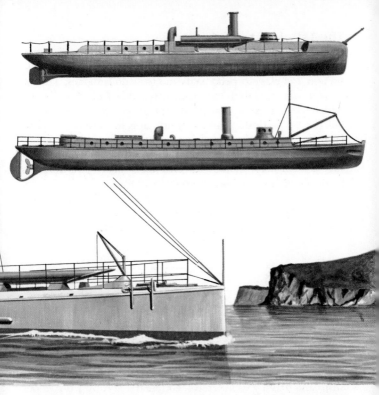

Most of the space in early torpedo craft was taken up by the boiler(s) and reciprocating machinery, with the conning position usually placed well aft. To improve forward vision the funnels were generally made as slim as possible and, as the only high points available, carried the steaming lights. Accommodation was crude (or non-existent) and a shelter, or cabin, was the usual provision for the crew during a twelve-hour operating period. The hull was generally made of wood for lightness but this was soon replaced by steel.

Naturally, such small and frail craft were very much at the mercy of the weather and could operate only in favourable conditions; but they could be built in large numbers and located at strategic points around the coast. They were potentially formidable craft, and made a close blockade by enemy naval forces so hazardous that it was soon discontinued.

The 1st class torpedo boat

Such was the demand for torpedo boats that their development was very rapid* and three main groups soon emerged: 1st and 2nd class torpedo boats and torpedo launches. The 1st class boats operated independently; the 2nd class boats, which were more restricted in operation, were sized to be hoisted by battleships and cruisers; and the smaller torpedo launches had to be carried by a parent ship to the scene of operations. The 1st class boat has survived, with variations, to the present day, while the 2nd class boats and torpedo launches became obsolete before the 1900s.

By about 1880 the 1st class boat had a high length/beam ratio and was flush decked with a turtle-backed fo'c'sle. There were generally two conning positions, one immediately abaft

the fo'c'sle, and one aft, with the machinery arranged amidships and driving twin screws. For greater accuracy torpedoes were now launched from a fixed bow tube (protected by the turtle-backed fo'c'sle) and training tubes mounted forward and/or aft of the after conning tower. When the craft was used as a torpedo boat, 3-pounder guns were mounted on the conning tower roofs, but heavier 6-pounder guns and machine guns could be shipped if torpedoes were not carried and the craft used as a gunboat against torpedo boats.

The torpedo gunboat

One of the many counters to early torpedo craft was the torpedo gunboat, which evolved from the torpedo boat's ability to ship either a gun or torpedo armament.

---

* For example, between 1874–91 no less than 222 torpedo boats were built at Chiswick by Thornycroft, commercial shipbuilders.

Two examples of later torpedo boats: the German *G.88* of 1898 (*above*) and the Spanish vessel *Arieté*, completed in 1887 (*below*)

The torpedo gunboat (TGB) was larger and more weatherly than the torpedo boat (TB), and carried a heavier, more numerous gun armament. Although faster, the gunboat was still too small to be effective, and it was made to look rather ridiculous by later, faster 1st class torpedo boats.

This was because all torpedo boat construction was in the hands of specialist private builders who naturally did not like to see their vessels countered by simple measures. Another factor was that the construction of all British torpedo gunboats had been allocated to the Royal Dockyards and private builders did not wish to lose their monopoly in fast light warships. It was, perhaps, no coincidence that the only British torpedo gunboat put out to private contract – the *Speedy* – made her designed speed while all others failed to do so.

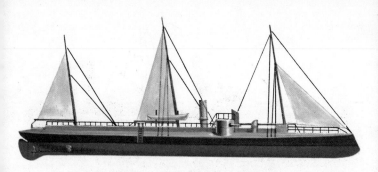

The British vessels had the first vertical triple expansion engines installed in warships and took steam at 150 lb/in^2 from four locomotive boilers. These engines were built to develop 3,000 ihp at natural draught and 4,000 ihp at forced draught for speeds of 19 and 21 knots respectively, but insufficient steam was generated at forced draught so that the designed speed was not attained. The exception was the *Speedy* which Thornycroft had provided with eight watertube boilers supplying an abundance of steam at 200 lb/in^2.

(*Above*) the French torpedo gunboat *Bombe* of 1887 and (*below*) the British *Speedy* (1894). Torpedo gunboats were built as the first counter to torpedo boat attack but in practice they were not fast enough to be successful.

One satisfactory feature of the torpedo gunboats was their seaworthiness, and as the weather worsened so their superiority over torpedo boats was made evident. Ironically, the degree of bad weather required was usually sufficient to keep torpedo boats in harbour.

The torpedo boat destroyer

Following the failure of the 450-ton torpedo gunboat to catch the 100-ton torpedo boat, it was proposed in 1892 that the machinery of the former be installed in an enlarged torpedo boat of about 250 tons to secure the high speed vitally lacking in the gunboat. The idea originated with Yarrow – one of the commercial specialist torpedo boat constructors – who shared the order for six prototype craft with Thornycroft and Laird. They were called torpedo boat destroyers (TBDs) – later abbreviated to destroyers – and were to steam at 27 knots and have a good gun armament.

The torpedo boat destroyer was similar, but larger and more seaworthy than the contemporary torpedo boat; however as most of the additional space was occupied by machinery there was little in the way of extra comfort for the crew. The armament comprised one 12-pounder gun on the roof of the

The French torpedo boat destroyer *Durandal* (1900) possessed the speed that torpedo gunboats lacked.

conning tower forward; three 6-pounder guns placed on each side abaft the turtle-backed fo'c'sle and aft; and one fixed bow tube and two single training tubes for 18-inch torpedoes. The bow tube was later discarded as it was of limited use and two extra 6-pounder guns were added amidships.

The torpedo boat destroyer emerged as a dual-function vessel which could accompany the fleet and provide it with a craft both sufficiently fast and well-armed to destroy contemporary torpedo boats; and it also replaced the latter for delivering torpedo attacks. Although torpedo boats were still built, mainly for minor navies with only coast defence commitments, major navies soon stopped building them altogether.

The ocean-going destroyer

While there was no denying the success of the first torpedo boat destroyers, they were only a little less fragile than the torpedo boats they replaced. However, as they had now become an integral part of the fleet, and were as necessary to it as the cruiser screen, it was essential that their seaworthiness be improved so that they could keep station with the fleet in all weathers.

A marked feature of the ocean-going destroyers that followed the turtle-backed torpedo boat destroyers in about 1900 was a more robust hull, heavier scantlings, and a short raised fo'c'sle, giving improved seaworthiness besides extra crew space. The conning tower in earlier torpedo boat destroyers had proved of little use as it was too low and vision was very limited; in fact the 12-pounder gun platform over it was more

frequently used at sea. Although the conning tower was still fitted in some of the new destroyers, it was backed by a chart room and wireless telegraphy office over which was a substantial open bridge that could comfortably accommodate and shelter the sea watch.

As a result of these improvements displacement was doubled and, although speed was nominally less in smooth water, this was more a theoretical than a practical disadvantage, as the earlier torpedo boat destroyers rapidly lost speed in a seaway. Initially there was no increase in armament but later destroyers sacrificed the 6-pounder guns for extra 12-pounders. Early models, such as the British 'River' class, were criticized

because they were larger, slower, and no better armed than their predecessors, but there was no complaint from sea as destroyer officers were well aware of the less obvious advantages of greater reliability, less maintenance, reduced discomfort for the crew, etc..

The turbine destroyer

The introduction of the steam turbine was a major step in destroyer development, and all early experimental work was undertaken in destroyers before turbine propulsion was extended to cruisers and battleships. Turbines offered economies in weight and space and naturally lent themselves to fast, light warships, but their high fuel consumption and high rate of revolution presented difficulties.

As early as 1900 experimental turbine destroyers were

Ocean-going destroyers: the British *Eden* of 1903 (*above*) and the American *Bainbridge* of 1902 (*below*)

reaching 35 knots with 10,000 shp, and this speed did not improve much over the next fifty years. The much larger power output required more steam so that economies in weight and space were offset by more boilers and, as they were still coal fired, increased engine room complement. The high revolutions of direct coupled turbines led to some odd screw arrangements because propeller diameter had to be kept small and required multiple screws on each shaft, while a reciprocating engine for cruising was proposed to extend the radius of action. All these setbacks were overcome by the provision of cruising turbines and reduction gearing for greater fuel economy and improved boiler performance, and later oil-firing substantially reduced the engine room complement.

By the beginning of the First World War the destroyer had advanced to nearly 1,000 tons displacement; it was powered by direct coupled turbines of 25,000 shp at a speed of 34 knots, taking steam at 250 lb/in^2 from three oil-fired boilers, was armed with three 4-inch guns and two twin 21-inch torpedo tubes, and could accompany the fleet practically anywhere. Two significant advances were made during the war: reduction gearing, installed experimentally prewar, was generally adopted, and superimposed guns were introduced.

The superimposition of guns
Most destroyers mounted their guns forward, amidships, and aft, so that while all could bear on the broadside there were wide arcs over bow and stern covered only by a single gun.

In 1916 the Royal Navy took the bold step with the 'V' and 'W' classes of shipping two guns forward and aft and superimposing the inner pair over the outer guns. This disposition had not been extended to destroyers earlier as the additional top weight was thought to impair stability. This was certainly not the case with the 'V's and 'W's and they were almost universally copied. For the next thirty years this arrangement remained a standard layout and it is a striking example of the basic simplicity underlying every good design.

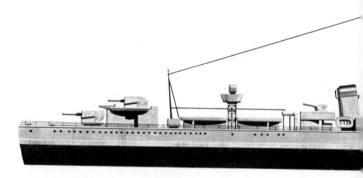

The coastal motor boat

In order to skim over minefields and attack enemy ships in their bases, the Royal Navy proposed in 1916 a boat not exceeding $4\frac{1}{4}$ tons in weight – so that it could be hoisted on a cruiser's davits – with a speed of about 30 knots and armed with an 18-inch torpedo. Only Thornycroft took up the tender, to which they could apply their experience with racing hydroplanes,* and the first coastal motor boats proved most successful. The weights for a typical boat were: hull $2\frac{1}{4}$ tons, machinery $\frac{3}{4}$ ton, and load (equipment, armament, fuel, etc.) 1 ton. Powered by a non-reversible 12-cylinder petrol engine of 250 bhp, the 40-foot boats attained 33 or 34 knots and launched their torpedoes tail-first over the stern.

*It is interesting to recall the first Royal Navy torpedo boat, the *Lightning*, was developed from the Thornycroft steam launch *Miranda* in 1871; and that another *Miranda* (IV), a hydroplane built in 1910, was the basis for coastal motor boat development.

Subsequent coastal motor boats were lengthened to 55 feet and 70 feet and the weight limitation had to be abandoned. The 55-foot boat had twin screws and, depending on the type of petrol engines installed, made between 32 and 40 knots and was armed with two torpedoes and four depth charges. The 70-foot boats were minelayers and could carry four 1-ton mines, but they made only 28½ knots (except one boat fitted with 24-cylinder petrol engines which made over 40 knots).

Similar triple screw boats were built in Germany and

Contemporary destroyer designs at the close of the First World War: the British 'V' class (*above*) and the American 'Wickes' class (*below*)

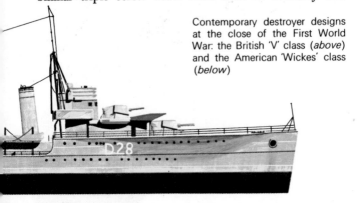

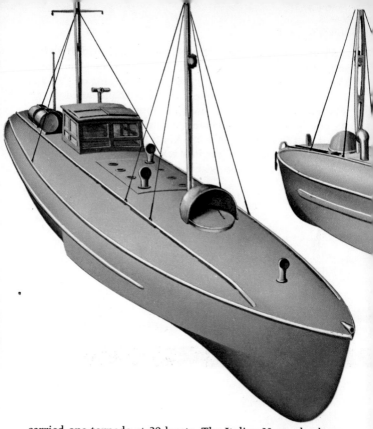

carried one torpedo at 30 knots. The Italian Navy also began
a large series of coastal motor boats which could be armed
either as minelayers (four mines), torpedo boats (two torpedoes in side-dropping gear), or gunboats (one 3-pounder
and machine guns) but were slower at 24 knots. One of these
boats, *MAS.15* (Rizzo), succeeded in sinking the Austro-
Hungarian battleship *Szent Istvan* in 1917 and made her
escape despite the presence of 30-knot destroyers.

The large destroyer

The practice of providing each destroyer flotilla with a more
powerfully armed leader of greater size dated back to the time
of the first ocean-going destroyers that could accompany the
fleet. From this came the idea of forming flotillas solely of

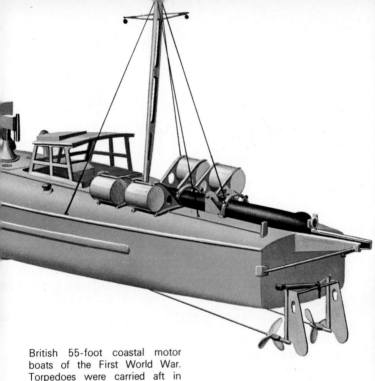

British 55-foot coastal motor boats of the First World War. Torpedoes were carried aft in a trough and were launched tail-first over the stern.

heavy destroyers to provide a concentration of force that could overwhelm all flotilla opposition. As such destroyers were expensive they were not initially built in large numbers, and they demonstrated the traditional tactic of an inferior fleet seeking to make up for small numbers with superior vessels. Thus, during the First World War, the German Navy produced destroyers armed with four 5·9-inch guns, but they were not outstandingly successful as too much had been attempted on the displacement. In the postwar years, however, the idea took root in many navies in many forms.

The smaller navies – such as those of Argentina, Spain, Yugoslavia, and Poland – had some powerful units built. The Argentine and Spanish destroyers were based on the Thornycroft flotilla leaders of the 'Shakespeare' class and were of

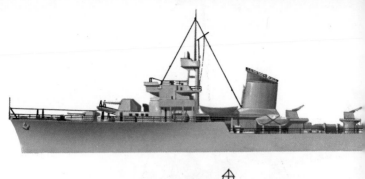

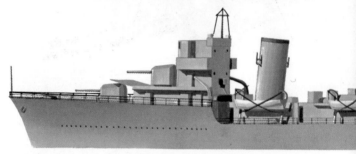

1,500 tons, capable of 36 knots, and armed with five 4·7-inch guns and six 21-inch torpedo tubes; the Yugoslav *Dubrovnik* was of 1,880 tons, capable of 37 knots, and armed with four 5·5-inch guns and six torpedo tubes; and the Polish *Blyska-wica* and *Grom* were of 1,975 tons, 39 knots, and armed with seven 4·7-inch guns and six torpedo tubes.

After the First World War the French Navy started on a large programme of heavy destroyers (the *contre-torpilleurs*). These vessels had developed from the '1,500-tonne' type of 1922, armed with four 5·1-inch guns and six 21·7-inch torpedo tubes and capable of 33 knots, to the '2,930-tonne' type of 1934, armed with eight 5·5-inch guns and ten 21·7-inch torpedo tubes and steaming at 39 knots.

As the first London Naval Treaty had imposed a total tonnage on destroyers, most major navies – the French being a singular exception – were inclined to spread this tonnage over more numerous destroyers of the standard type; but all of them built small groups of heavy destroyers. Thus, the Italian Navy built two series of heavy units of about 1,600 tons (six or eight 4·7-inch guns); the Royal Navy the 'Tribal' class

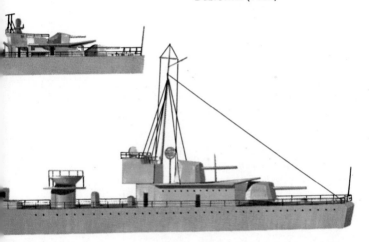

Two large destroyers, both British-built: (*above*) the Polish *Grom* and (*below*) the Yugoslav *Dubrovnik* (1932)

of 1,870 tons (eight 4·7-inch guns); and the United States Navy the 'Porter' class of 1,850 tons (eight 5-inch guns): all these vessels had heavy gun armaments.

For a while Japan also followed this policy, but in 1925 she started the 'Fubuki' class of 1,700 tons (actually of over 2,000 tons) and 34 knots, which were armed with six 5-inch guns and nine torpedo tubes. The latter were thought to be for standard 21-inch torpedoes but much later it was found that they were for the greatly improved 24-inch torpedoes used with such telling effect during the Second World War. When the German Navy embarked on destroyer construction in 1934 it also turned to heavy units for its small flotilla, and its 1,600-ton (actually over 2,200-ton) vessels carried five 5-inch guns and eight 21-inch torpedo tubes which, like the Japanese units, were provided with reloads.

The motor torpedo boat

Between the wars the coastal motor boats languished, and relatively few craft were built. However, from about 1935 Germany, Italy and Great Britain showed fresh interest.

To its great advantage, the Germany Navy possessed a light-weight diesel engine system and was able to build robust round-bilge craft of little over a hundred tons, capable of 35 knots and of carrying four torpedoes. The stepped boat of limited seaworthiness was preferred by the Italian Navy and, at 24 tons, it could carry two torpedoes at 42 knots. For improved seaworthiness the Royal Navy abandoned the stepped coastal motor boat and built a hard-chine boat of 22 tons, 33 knots, and with two torpedoes. In the United Kingdom there was a marked rivalry between two commercial firms, British Power Boat and Vosper, and although the latter eventually secured the Admiralty contract for motor torpedo boats (MTB),* the former took their craft across to the United States where it was accepted as the prototype for the American patrol torpedo (PT) boat.

* On the other hand British Power Boat secured the Admiralty contract for motor anti-submarine boats (MA/SB) and the subsequent motor gunboats (MGB) developed from them.

Standard British 70-foot motor torpedo boat in service at the outbreak of the Second World War, with fixed deck tubes for launching torpedoes

All boats were of wood construction and – except in Germany – powered by petrol engines; they were therefore very prone to fire and explosion. Although more seaworthy than the coastal motor boat, the motor torpedo boat was still hampered by weather restrictions and lacked suitable light guns and equipment. Its presence was usually revealed by its unsilenced engines; later a separate low-powered engine was provided for silent attack but its low speed proved impractical.

War construction

From the outbreak of the Second World War destroyer construction was made a high priority in all navies. The Royal Navy immediately reverted to the standard type to speed production, and a feature of all war designs was a marked increase in anti-aircraft fire. The German Navy continued with its heavy destroyers and for a short period substituted 5·9-inch for 5-inch guns. It planned some interesting projects with diesel main propulsion but none was ever completed.

All French construction came to a halt after the surrender in 1940. The Italian Navy pursued a line similar to that of the Royal Navy. Japan also progressed vigorously with a rather heavy standard destroyer and, like Germany, would have been better served by a larger number of smaller units.

All other destroyer construction was overshadowed by the size of the United States' war effort, and once the prewar backlog was cleared production switched to two large standard designs. The earlier 'Fletcher' class of 2,050 tons made 37 knots and were armed with five 5-inch guns and ten 21-inch

torpedo tubes, while the later 'Allen M. Sumner' and 'Gearing' classes ran to 2,200 and 2,425 tons, 36½ knots, and were armed with six 5-inch guns and ten torpedo tubes. No less than 410 destroyers of these classes were authorized, although the end of the war caused sixty cancellations.

The destroyer escort

Although it was not the most suitable vessel for anti-submarine and anti-aircraft escort duties, the destroyer was mainly used for this purpose because it was the only type of vessel available in large numbers. However, even before the war the Royal Navy had already decided that a destroyer used for escort duties could be smaller, slower, and less complex than the fleet unit, and could therefore be produced more rapidly and at less cost. Consequently the small prewar programme was continued until 1942 when the even simpler frigate was put into production. Both the United States and Japan came to share this opinion, but Japan only began production in 1943 after suffering heavy losses with fleet destroyers.

These pictures show how funnels, once the epitome of speed, have gradually decreased in number. (*From the left, top to bottom*) American 'Wickes' class of 1916 with four funnels; a French 'Jaguar' class of 1924 (three funnels); a British 'G' class with two (1936), and an Italian 'Oriani' class (1937) with one funnel

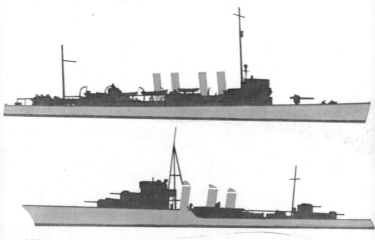

The three designs were in no way similar: the British units were small destroyers; the American vessels had a distinctive profile and the slower units had diesel-electric, and the faster units turbo-electric, propulsion; whereas the Japanese vessels had severe utility lines similar to their sloops.

Both the German and Italian navies had built torpedo boats* before the war, and they continued to build them during the war as a type of small destroyer. The torpedo boat, however, while smaller and cheaper than the destroyer, and possessing many of its refinements, lacked the destroyer escort's essential simplicity, an important factor in production.

The fast patrol boat

Developments in many fields enabled light naval craft to become very effective small fighting units in the postwar years. The gas turbine gave high speed from a compact and lightweight power unit, and as an alternative there was the lightweight diesel engine. In addition a wide selection of light, compact and highly reliable weapon, detection, and electronic systems became available so that light naval craft could be armed and equipped for specialist roles.

* Both navies were limited to 600 tons for these vessels by treaty: the German Navy under the Versailles Treaty and the Italian Navy under the London Naval Treaty which placed no limitation on vessels of 600 tons and under.

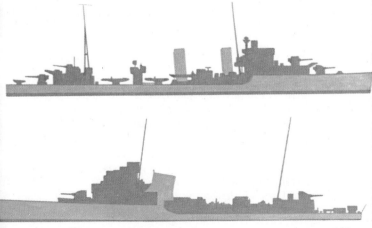

Gas turbine powered torpedo boats: the Swedish *Spica* (*above*) of 1966; (*below*) the *Brave Swordsman*, a British vessel (1958)

During the Second World War coastal forces included motor torpedo boats, motor gunboats, motor launches, etc., but now classed as fast patrol boats of three main types:-

(a) the steel round-bilge form gunboat powered by either gas turbines or diesel engines;

(b) the wood hard-chine convertible torpedo boat/gunboat/minelayer/raiding craft with gas turbines for high-speed propulsion; and

(c) the steel round-bilge form patrol boat with diesel propulsion and a large radius of action.

As the gas turbine has a higher fuel consumption than the diesel engine the choice between them for high-speed craft is determined by the radius of action required, as beyond a certain point it is more economic to install the heavier diesel engine with lower fuel consumption. Round-bilge form craft can be fitted with fin stabilization to make them more seaworthy than their wartime counterparts. Fin stabilization and gas turbines have widened the scope of fast patrol boats so considerably that the present-day 100-ton craft have a capability equalled by few 1,000-ton prewar vessels.

Gun-armed destroyers such as the Soviet 'Skory' class vessel (*above*) of 1949 have now been supplemented by missile-armed destroyers; an example is the American 'Charles F. Adams' class (*below*) dating from 1960.

The missile destroyer

As a type the destroyer, like the cruiser, has ceased to exist, since the categories that applied to conventional warfare hardly suit modern conflict. Therefore the current missile destroyer is no more than a missile-armed vessel of destroyer size. If it was larger, or smaller, it would be loosely called a missile cruiser or missile frigate. An anomaly arises here as the United States Navy realistically rates frigates above destroyers, while vessels below destroyer size are classed as escorts and were developed from the destroyer escort.

Only the Soviet Union built large numbers of conventional destroyers after the war. They were fine examples of their type and politically they have served the Soviet Navy well.

Most missile destroyers have a combined main propulsion plant comprising long-life steam turbines for cruising and gas turbines for high speed; moreover, the gas turbine can be rapidly under way from the shut-down condition. The missile armament usually includes both long-range and short-range anti-aircraft missiles, supplemented by a gun system for bombardment purposes and an anti-submarine weapon with a helicopter. This armament is accompanied by extensive radar installations, as there would be little point in providing long-range missiles without a matching sea and air guard.

Considerable space is taken up by the computers and test gear associated with the missile systems, and by the extensive communications equipment required for modern warships. Naturally, there is a heavy demand for electricity and the generating capacity of the British 'County' class is typical: two 1,000-kilowatt alternators (powered by steam turbines), two 500-kilowatt alternators (powered by gas turbines) and a 750-kilowatt emergency set, also powered by a gas turbine. They can be shut down in areas contaminated with nuclear fall-out by withdrawing the crew in exposed positions to the gas-tight citadel supplied with filtered air, from which the main machinery can be kept under remote control.

British submarine *No. 1* (1902) of the 'Holland' type, running on the surface

SUBMARINES

The Holland submarine

The submarine developed from the need for a craft that could submerge to avoid detection when attacking. However, early submarine craft were technically ahead of their time because there were no effective means of propulsion or of navigating when submerged, and nor were suitable weapons available. Early submarines were therefore small and manually propelled, and the usual method of attack was to attach an explosive charge to an anchored warship.

The submarine developed into an effective combatant craft when the internal combustion engine became available for surface propulsion and was allied with electric propulsion while submerged, and when a torpedo armament, and the periscope and gyrocompass for navigation, had been evolved. This combination of events occurred in about 1900, and, although there were successful submarines before this date,

they all lacked one, or more, of the essentials mentioned above.

For this reason the American-designed Holland submarines are generally considered the earliest effective craft of this type, and many foreign navies – including those of Austria-Hungary, Great Britain, Italy, Japan, and Russia – adopted the Holland design for their first submarines. The first Holland boat for the United States Navy was a coast defence unit of limited radius which displaced only 120 tons submerged. The cylindrical hull was of full form and was divided into three main compartments: the torpedo room forward, the control room amidships, and the engine room aft. The two forward compartments were further divided by a deck to provide tank and battery spaces below. A small conning tower was fitted amidships, and, forward of it, was the externally mounted magnetic compass. When attacking, the boat had to break surface at intervals, so that the target could be kept under observation because the vessel ran blind when submerged; but a periscope fitted to the British boats of this

type enabled the target to be tracked while submerged. Main propulsion was by a 160 bhp petrol engine and a 70 shp electric motor (which the batteries could supply for four hours), coupled to a single shaft. The armament comprised a fixed tube in the bow for 14-inch torpedoes, and two or four reloads were carried internally. There was little in the way of comfort for the crew of seven but this was acceptable because of the boat's limited radius of operation.

Developments up to 1914

Until the outbreak of the First World War submarine development was rapid, and succeeding classes increased in size and scope of employment. Not even the battlefleet at sea was considered safe from attack, and having survived the threat of surface torpedo attack the capital ship was now confronted with the same attack from an unseen assailant. The control of areas of strategic importance, such as the North Sea and the Mediterranean, was therefore disputed when battleships came to be opposed by submarines.

Although Germany lagged behind other major navies in adopting submarines she introduced first the heavy oil, and then the diesel, engine which completely replaced petrol motors for surface propulsion. Besides eliminating the danger of explosion prevalent with petrol vapour, the higher output and greater fuel economy of the diesel engine advanced the submarine to an ocean-going craft, and this placed further restrictions on major surface units. Thus, by the outbreak of war, submarines had reached the dimensions and performance summarized in Table 1 on page 126.

However, the above comparisons tend to be misleading as not all navies had reached the same stage in submarine development, and neither did all the boats listed achieve designed performance. It is worth noting that all boats shipped one or more deck guns with the exception of the Russian craft which shipped external launching gear for torpedoes on deck.

(*Opposite*) British 'D' class submarine (1910). (*Above*) 'K' class fleet submarine (1917)

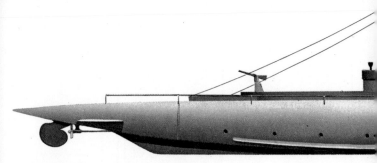

Submarine warfare 1914-8

An untried weapon at the start of the First World War, the submarine rapidly established its position when the German *U.9* sank three British armoured cruisers proceeding in company off the Dutch coast in September 1914. However, it was when the German Navy used its submarines against merchant shipping that the greatest damage was done. By 1917 the Allied position was so serious that – with great armies locked in stalemate on land – the submarine came close to deciding the issue at sea in favour of Germany. Allied countermeasures and the convoy system finally prevailed and the high casualty rate was halted. Nonetheless, the mercantile losses were appalling, and about 2,500 vessels (excluding fishing craft) totalling nearly 12,000,000 tons gross were destroyed by submarines during this period.

During the war the German Navy embarked on the construction of 766 submarines, which fell into four main groups:-

    (a) medium-sized sea-going (U-) boats;

(b) coastal (UB- and UF-) boats;

(c) sea-going (U-) and coastal (UC-) boats for minelaying; and

(d) submarine cruisers.

Against merchant shipping German submarines used the gun more often than the torpedo, and the submarine cruisers – mounting two 5·9-inch guns – were designed more for gun than torpedo action. Although 419 submarines were not completed, the balance – together with the forty-five boats ordered prewar – absorbed the greater proportion of Allied naval strength.

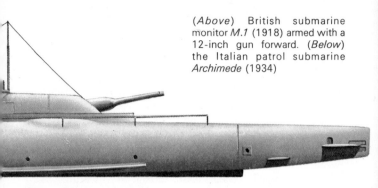

(*Above*) British submarine monitor *M.1* (1918) armed with a 12-inch gun forward. (*Below*) the Italian patrol submarine *Archimede* (1934)

The steam submarine

Before the introduction of the internal combustion engine most early submarines had to use steam for surface propulsion. Although it was surprising to see it reintroduced during the First World War by the Royal Navy, it was understandable in view of the speed and power output required by a fleet submarine. Exaggerated reports of the high surface speed of German submarines made the British Admiralty believe that the German Navy already possessed fleet submarines, and that therefore they must be provided for the British fleet.

To work with the fleet a sustained speed of 21 knots was required, and as the preceding 'J' class submarines had fallen 2 knots below this figure with diesel engines pushed to their utmost, there was no alternative but steam.

The 'K' class displaced 2,650 tons submerged, were 338 feet long, and were powered by geared turbines developing 10,000 shp at a surface speed of 24 knots. A narrow superstructure amidships supported a small wheelhouse and two hinged funnels; the armament comprised 4-inch guns at each end of the superstructure, a 3-inch anti-aircraft gun between the wheelhouse and fore funnel, and ten 18-inch torpedo tubes

disposed four forward, four amidships, and two in a twin external mounting enclosed by the superstructure.

Auxiliary surface propulsion was by an 800 bhp diesel generator supplying power to the electric motors; these enabled the steam plant to be shut and diving accomplished more rapidly given early warning of an enemy approach.

In all, twenty-seven units were ordered – *K.1-21* and *K.23-28*; *K.13*, which sank on trials, was later salvaged and renumbered *K.22*. They had an unhappy history: six were lost (all by accident), five cancelled, four converted while building into submarine monitors, and the remainder ultimately scrapped. Their least satisfactory features were unhandiness when submerged and the length of time required to dive, but they easily made their speed on the surface and were reasonable seaboats with careful handling. Ironically, the close of the war revealed that the German Navy possessed no fleet submarines; nor had it planned any.

The submarine monitor

As the British submarine generally had to close to within 1,000 yards to secure a hit with the torpedo, and was frequently unable to do so owing to target movement and the submarine's low speed when submerged, it was proposed to arm the vessel with a heavy gun which would make it possible to engage targets at a considerably greater range.

Four uncompleted vessels of the 'K' class – *K. 18-21* which were renumbered as *M.1-4* – were selected for this purpose

and were armed with 12-inch guns removed from old battle-ships; these could be laid and trained through twenty degrees, but could be loaded only on the surface. The vessels were powered by diesel engines, and were consequently shorter than the 'K' class as the boiler room could be omitted; they retained the torpedo armament fitted in the bows.

They passed through their trials satisfactorily and the 12-inch gun presented no difficulties. The British Admiralty, however, thought that Germany might well copy the sub-marine monitor, and was reluctant to introduce a weapon which might prove more damaging to the Royal Navy than the enemy. Consequently, construction was slowed down and the *M.4*, which was the least advanced, was cancelled. Only the *M.1* was completed before the end of hostilities, and she was sent to the Mediterranean away from prying German eyes.

The patrol submarine

After the First World War most navies concentrated on the construction of sea-going patrol submarines based on such successful and war-proven craft as the medium-sized British 'L' and German 'U.81' classes.

More attention was given to submarine qualities such as rapid diving, good torpedo armament, the provision of re-loads, and increased underwater radius; to good surface qualities which would maintain an adequate sustained speed; and to more reliable equipment. So, while performance was not spectacular, overall capability improved significantly.

The German coastal submarine *U.9* (1936)

Patrol submarines ranged between 1,000 and 1,500 tons, made 16 to 18 knots on the surface, and were generally armed with one 4-inch or 4·7-inch gun, four or six bow tubes and two stern torpedo tubes. The French and Netherlands navies both preferred to carry most of the torpedo tubes externally in trainable mountings, but the more usual practice was to fit them internally where they could be reloaded. During the 1930s, however, many submarines added fixed external tubes to increase their attacking power. The British 'T' class, for example, were provided with eleven torpedo tubes of which five were fitted externally. Although the double hull was sometimes preferred for the larger boats, the single hull with saddle tanks was widely adopted. The conning tower was sited about amidships and forward and aft of it a free-flooding deck casing extended to the ends. Stout jumper wires ran from the stem and stern to the periscope standard so that any underwater obstructions rode over the gun(s) and conning tower.

Although American and Japanese patrol submarines were invariably larger than their European counterparts, Japan also built smaller patrol craft of under 1,000 tons for work in the narrow seas. Coastal boats of about 250 tons were built only by those navies with specific requirements for them.

The submarine cruiser

For a short period after the First World War there was considerable interest in submarine cruisers because of the performance of the German 'U.131' and 'U.139' classes. The interest was understandable in Japan and the United States, both bordered by the vast Pacific Ocean, but less so in other navies, particularly those of Europe. Whereas Japan continued to build this type right up to and through the Second World War, the United States soon abandoned it and started fresh development with smaller patrol submarines. Brief details of some American and Japanese submarine cruisers are given in Table 2 on page 127.

Great Britain and France also built a few submarine cruisers but did not continue this type. The French *Surcouf* was particularly interesting. The vessel had a submerged displacement of 4,304 tons and a surface speed of $18\frac{1}{2}$ knots; she was armed with two 8-inch guns in a twin turret and eight 21·7-inch and four 15·7-inch torpedo tubes, and carried a seaplane and a light boarding boat (this was later removed). The British *X.1* was more conventional and on 3,600 tons (submerged) could make $19\frac{1}{2}$ knots on the surface; she was armed with four 5·2-inch guns in twin turrets and six 21-inch

The German patrol submarine
U.26 (1936)

torpedo tubes. Although both Britain and France possessed numerous overseas bases, neither of them envisaged a large-scale war involving mercantile interests, and the submarine cruiser – which was costly to build – was not a high priority.

During the Second World War the Japanese Navy embarked on a series of large submarines which were designed to act as

command centres for its scouting and raiding squadrons. The 'I.400' class had a radius of 30,000 miles at $16\frac{1}{2}$ knots and surpassed even the *Surcouf* in size. On deck was a large hangar able to accommodate three torpedo/bomber aircraft with a catapult arranged along the fore-deck; the conning tower was offset to port over the hangar.

The minelaying submarine

During the First World War the submarine showed that it was the only type of warship able to operate in enemy controlled waters, and this drove home the point that to date enemy forces had exercised only a surface control. The shallow waters of the North Sea – and the continental shelf generally – were very suitable for mining, and the German Navy was first in the field with its small minelayers (or UC-boats); these

(*Above*) the British submarine cruiser *X.1* (1926). (*Below*) the French submarine cruiser *Surcouf* (1932)

undertook lays all round the United Kingdom coast and could work well inshore. The first UC-boats entered service in mid-1915 and, displacing only 183 tons submerged, they carried twelve mines in six mine shafts forward. Nearly 200 of these craft were projected during the war, of which more than half

were put into service, and the final units displaced 564 tons submerged and were armed with one 3·5-inch or 4·1-inch gun and three 19·7-inch torpedo tubes besides stowing fourteen mines.

The British effort was later and much smaller, and initially special mines were developed which submarines could discharge through the standard torpedo tube. Later, during 1916, external mine shafts were provided in six 'E' class submarines, but no special minelaying submarines were built during the course of the war.

Between the wars most navies built small classes of minelaying submarines, and the German Navy developed a submarine mine that would fit the standard 21-inch torpedo tube so that virtually any of its boats could be used for minelaying when the occasion arose. Submarine mining was not so intensive during the Second World War as aircraft could undertake lays in enemy waters. Minelaying submarines generally carried their mines in free-flooding shafts, whether they were fitted externally or internally, so that the pressure hulls remained watertight.

The 'true' submarine

In actual fact the submarine was misnamed. The craft would have been more correctly described if the word 'submersible' had been chosen, denoting one that could submerge but spent most of its time on the surface.

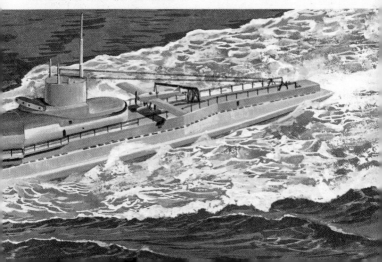

During the Second World War the German Navy mounted a submarine attack against mercantile shipping on a scale that far surpassed its campaign during the First World War. To some extent this was countered by greatly improved anti-submarine measures which were vitally supported by aircraft. What finally turned the scales in favour of the anti-submarine forces was the fitting of search radar to aircraft (it was already installed in ships), so that they were no longer dependent on visual sightings and could press home attacks by day or night, in clear weather or reduced visibility.

To survive, the submarine had to remain submerged, but for this purpose the conventional battery-driven electric motors were quite inadequate in both speed and radius. The long-term answer lay in developing a suitable closed-cycle engine which did not require air, but in the interim the German Navy introduced two short-term measures:-

(a) the *schnorchel** or air mast, which up to a depth of about thirty feet enabled the main diesel engines to be run; and
(b) the all-electric boat, which had the battery capacity

* Anglicized to snort.

trebled and also incorporated the snort into the design.

The latter had diesel-electric propulsion when using the air mast – the diesel engines drove generators which supplied power to the electric motors – instead of direct diesel drive, but when going deep the batteries supplied the power in the usual way. As the craft was designed to carry out a patrol completely submerged all surface characteristics could be dropped and the hull shaped for optimum under-water performance. This slim, streamlined, deep hull, with a figure-of-eight cross-section, was first in a new generation of 'true' submarines.

The resulting type XXI submarine had a submerged displacement of 1,819 tons, a submerged speed of 16 knots, and was armed with six 21-inch torpedo tubes and seventeen reloads. It was silent running, hard to detect and consequently difficult to destroy, but it was put into production too late to halt the German slide to defeat.

Despite intensive effort the German Navy was not successful in producing a closed-cycle engine, but it came close to it with the Walter system whereby the thermal energy produced by the decomposition of a high concentration of hydrogen peroxide was sufficient to turn a turbine. Although a large

(*Above*) the Dutch minelaying submarine *0.19* (1939). (*Below*) the German submarine *U.793* (1944)

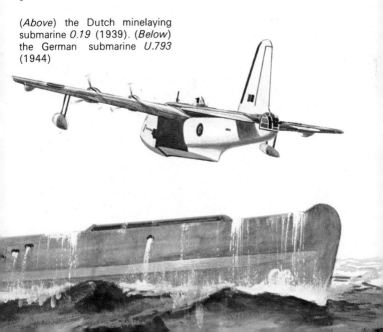

The British submarine *Excalibur* (1958)

number of Walter boats were planned, only a few actually entered service and the Royal Navy – with two postwar experimental craft – was only a little more successful.

The midget submarine

These craft were built for specific operations, tasks which it would be difficult to envisage until hostilities had actually commenced unless, as in the case of Japan, a surprise attack was intended. The origin of these special attack craft lay back in the First World War with the Italian *Grillo,* a marine tank.

Before the Second World War only the Italian and Japanese navies had undertaken the construction of midget submarines for entering enemy harbours and these had to be carried to the scene of operations by parent craft. In 1942 the Royal Navy started a series of midget craft to attack the German capital ships which lay in Norwegian fjords and threatened the Atlantic and Arctic convoy routes. The British craft was completely different from the enemy type because it was towed to the operating area and armed with explosive charges which were attached to the target's hull, whereas both the Italian and Japanese craft were carried on deck by a parent submarine and were armed with torpedo tubes, although the Italian craft was later altered to carry charges instead of torpedoes.

In 1944 the German Navy started a large series of midget craft for anti-invasion purposes, and although it was originally planned that these craft should carry a single mine, this was changed to an underslung torpedo, and a later series carried two underslung torpedoes.

In addition, all the above navies developed various types of manned torpedoes. The British and Italian types were similar and had a detachable warhead for securing to the target's hull, whereas the German and Japanese types were used as conventional torpedoes. No means of escape was provided for the pilot in the Japanese models.

The nuclear submarine

On 17 January 1955, the signal lamp on the American submarine *Nautilus* flashed the following message: 'Under way on nuclear power.'. Thus, within a decade that saw the advent of the atomic age, this new source of power was harnessed and controlled for ship propulsion.

Although the German type XXI boats had come as close to the true submarine as conventional propulsion allowed, the *Nautilus* can operate completely divorced from the atmosphere. Her closed-cycle nuclear plant gives her a practically unlimited radius of action, and the air in the boat is kept fresh by being continually circulated through a regenerative plant. In case of a power failure there is an auxiliary propulsion plant – a back-up system which is colloquially referred to as 'belt-and-braces' in the United States Navy – comprising an electric motor drawing power from either a small bank of batteries or a diesel generator set; an air mast is provided for the generator.

The American nuclear-powered submarine *George Washington* (1959)

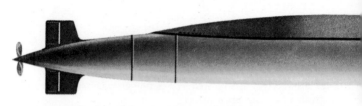

Now truly a vehicle of the deep, the nuclear-powered submarine adopted the full hull-form best suited to totally submerged operation, and the streamlined fin is fitted to enclose the periscope standards, masts for radar, communications, and position fixing, and the snort. She must 'surface' – this entails coming to a depth which allows the appropriate mast to break the surface of the water – only to receive (or send) wireless telegraphy messages or to fix her position. With all surface characteristics eliminated the best propulsion is obtained by a single large diameter screw turning at low revolutions, with steering rudders placed above and below it.

The missile submarine
The nuclear-powered submarine came to play an important part in the intercontinental ballistic missile system because its

great mobility and elusiveness make it a launch pad far superior to the hard-pad missile sites ashore.

The missile-armed submarine differed fundamentally from other warships in that it was not designed to fight ships at all, but to deliver an attack with the American Polaris missile on strategic enemy points up to 2,500 miles away; the distance has now been extended to 3,500 miles with the Poseidon missile. The submarine, however, is also fitted with conventional torpedo tubes.

At the present time the missile submarine represents the ultimate deterrent. Impervious to satellite surveillance, it is nevertheless vitally dependent on communications. However, an inertial navigation system has to some extent replaced external methods of position fixing, and the nuclear submarine's ability to go under polar ice broke the last ocean barrier.

(*Above*) the nuclear-powered and missile-armed French submarine *Redoutable* (1969). (*Below*) conning tower and gun armament of the Italian patrol submarine *Barbarigo* (1938)

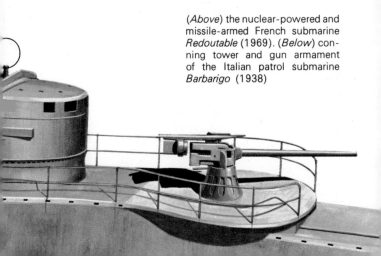

A Japanese 'I.400' class submarine cruiser (1940)

Table 1: submarine development by 1914 (see page 108)

CLASS	DISPLACE-MENT	HP & SPEED	ARMAMENT Guns	TTs●
'U.VII' Austro-Hungarian	810/930 tons	bhp 2,300 shp 1,260 = 16/10½ knots	1 × 4·1 in.	5 × 17·7 in.
'Diane' French	630/945 tons	bhp 1,800 shp* = 18½/11 knots	4 × 65 mm.	10 × 17·7 in.
'U.19' German	650/837 tons	bhp 1,700 shp 1,200 = 15/9½ knots	1 × 3·5 in.	4 × 19·7 in.
'E' British	725/810 tons	bhp 1,600 shp 840 = 16/10 knots	1 × 12 pdr.	5 × 18 in.
'Balilla' Italian	728/875 tons	bhp 1,300 shp 450 = 14/9 knots	2 × 3 in.	4 × 17·7 in.
'I.16' Japanese	520/900 tons	bhp 2,100 shp 1,000 = 17½/9 knots	1 × 3 in.	6 × 18 in.
'Nerpa' Russian	630/758 tons	bhp 500 shp 900 = 11/9 knots	12 × 17·7 in. 4 int. 8 ext.	
'L' American	450/548 tons	bhp 900 shp 680 = 14/10½ knots	1 × 3 in.	4 × 18 in.

*No information available   †submerged   ●torpedo tubes

Table 2: submarine cruisers (see page 115).

CLASS	DISPLACE-MENT†	HP & SPEED	ARMAMENT			
			Guns TTs●		Aircraft	Mines
'I.51' (1921) Japanese	2,430 tons	bhp 5,200 shp 2,000 = 20/10 knots	1 × 4·7 in. 1 × 3 in. 8 × 21 in.	—	—	—
'I.1' (1924) Japanese	2,791 tons	bhp 6,000 shp 2,600 = 18/8 knots	2 × 5·5 in. 6 × 21 in.	—	—	—
'I.13' (1944) Japanese	4,762 tons	bhp 4,400 shp 1,200 = 16½/5½ knots	1 × 5·5 in. 6 × 21 in.		2	—
'I.400' (1944) Japanese	6,560 tons	bhp 7,200 shp 2,400 = 18/6½ knots	1 × 5·5 in. 8 × 21 in.		3	—
'V.1' (1924) American	2,620 tons	bhp 6,700 shp 2,400 = 18/11 knots	1 × 5 in. 6 × 21 in.	—		—
'V.4' (1927) American	4,080 tons	bhp 3,175 shp 2,400 = 15/8 knots	2 × 6 in. 4 × 21 in.	—		80
'V.5' (1929) American	4,050 tons	bhp 5,450 shp 2,540 = 17/8 knots	2 × 6 in. 6 × 21 in.	—		—

The British gunboat *Redwing* (1881) in action

SLOOPS

Sloops and gunboats

Following the general introduction of steam, smaller naval vessels were loosely termed sloops and gunboats, and although their characteristics were ill-defined they were usually under 1,000 tons and adhered to wood construction (for cheapness) and to the full rig (as their bunker capacity was naturally limited) long after their larger and more combatant contemporaries had abandoned them. Those navies with large overseas commitments found them invaluable for flag-showing purposes and for preserving national dignity: the usual reaction to any report of trouble was to 'send a gunboat'.

The earliest gunboats were flush decked with a high gunwale and on the centre-line they carried two large slide-mounted smooth-bore guns which were shifted to ports on the engaged side by means of deck races. Later gunboats, like the sloops, had a fo'c'sle and poop and still carried the heavier guns on traversing slides on the centre-line but with the addition of lighter guns at broadside ports. They generally had a three-masted fore-and-aft rig with the funnel stepped between the foremast and mainmast. Originally conned from the poop, they gradually adopted a bridge sited forward of the funnel.

Sloops and gunboats passed from wood to composite, and then to steel, construction in the 1860-70s and carried breech-loading guns on central pivot mountings on the broadside, generally arranged two on the fo'c'sle, two or four in the waist, and two on the poop. Until 1900 they were built in large numbers as instruments of colonial expansion, but after the turn of the century severe reductions were made. As naval rivalry increased there was a natural reluctance to spend money on vessels of little combatant value. In addition, the introduction of wireless telegraphy permitted faster communication and a more centralized control over dispersed naval units, and this led to a reduction in the number of sloops and gunboats. By 1914 these vessels were considered obsolete, although several still remained in service.

The First World War, however, amply demonstrated that even total war had many side-shows in which sloops and gunboats could be extremely useful. By 1918 the submarine

Profile of *Redwing*

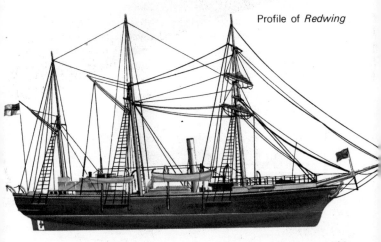

(*Above*) the German gunboat *Iltis* (1898). (*Below*) the British sloop *Cadmus* (1904)

threat to mercantile shipping had re-established the sloop as a convoy escort, and the vessel also proved itself invaluable for minesweeping: a new lease of life in two essential roles was ensured.

The 'Flower' class sloop

Late in 1914 the pressing need for minesweepers induced the British Admiralty to order a dozen light draught vessels. To speed their construction the design was made simple, and it conformed largely with mercantile practice so that the orders could be placed with shipyards that did not specialize in naval work. The result was the 'Flower' class sloops, which proved most successful, versatile, and reliable; and by the end of the war over one hundred of them had been built for the British and French navies. Although intended for minesweeping they were mainly employed in anti-submarine and patrol work and displayed good sea-keeping qualities.

With a vertical stem (strengthened for ramming), a fo'c'sle, and two slim funnels, these handsome vessels were powered by reciprocating engines turning a single screw for a speed of 16 knots. The armament comprised two 12-pounder guns, altered to 4-inch or 4·7-inch guns in later units, and – bearing in mind the vessels were designed as minesweepers – the magazine was placed right aft. Some units were modified to resemble merchant ships (Q-ships) and had their armament concealed behind lidded ports.

The sloop between the wars

Although seldom so-classed, vessels with sloop characteristics continued to be built after the First World War as either escorts or minesweepers: two very similar types which were, in fact, interchangeable. While practically all navies needed minesweepers, only those which had to maintain sea communications, and this invariably meant the navies of the colonial powers, built escort sloops.

The Royal Navy built more sloops than other navies as it was heavily committed to protecting British trade. The new vessels were just as useful as the 'Flower' class they replaced but had turbine propulsion and shallower draught. In 1930 the first London Naval Treaty defined a sloop as a vessel not exceeding (a) a displacement of 2,000 tons, (b) a speed of 20 knots, and (c) an armament of four 6-inch guns and no torpedo tubes. Only the United States Navy built up to this limit – the sloops *Charleston* and *Erie* – but the

French closely approached it with the 1,969-ton 'Bougainville' class which made $15\frac{1}{2}$ knots on diesel engines, were armed with three 5·5-inch guns, fitted for minelaying, and carried an aircraft.

By the outbreak of the Second World War the

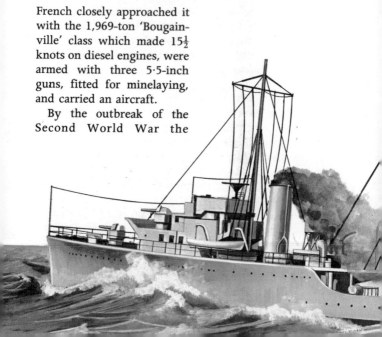

The Siamese escort sloop *Tachin* (1937)

British ocean escort sloop had advanced to a vessel of 1,250 tons, 19 knots, and eight 4-inch anti-aircraft guns in four twin mountings; the minesweeping sloop had

not increased in size and was of under 1,000 tons, 16 knots, and two single 4-inch anti-aircraft guns; and a new coastal escort sloop had been introduced of under 600 tons

The Australian escort sloop *Yarra* (1935)

(there were no treaty restrictions on vessels under this tonnage), 20 knots, and one 4-inch gun.

War construction

Even before the outbreak of the Second World War the Royal Navy realized that it faced a critical shortage in escorts, and that existing designs – good as they were – were unsuitable for series production in the United Kingdom. Therefore, drawing on its experience in the First World War, the British Admiralty sought a commercial prototype which would meet minimum naval requirements. Smiths Dock (Middlesbrough) proposed a modification of their whale-catcher *Southern Pride*, and this was accepted. Large orders were again placed with yards that did not specialize in naval work, and the vessels passed into service as 'Flower' class corvettes. Of 925 tons they steamed at 16 knots with reciprocating machinery, and were armed with one 4-inch gun and anti-submarine equipment.

Although it performed yeoman service the corvette proved a little too small for ocean work, and was replaced in 1942 by the larger and faster twin-screw 'River' class frigates. So that production could be speeded still further the design of the frigate was slightly altered to suit prefabricated construction,

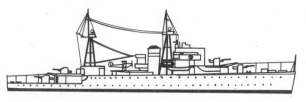

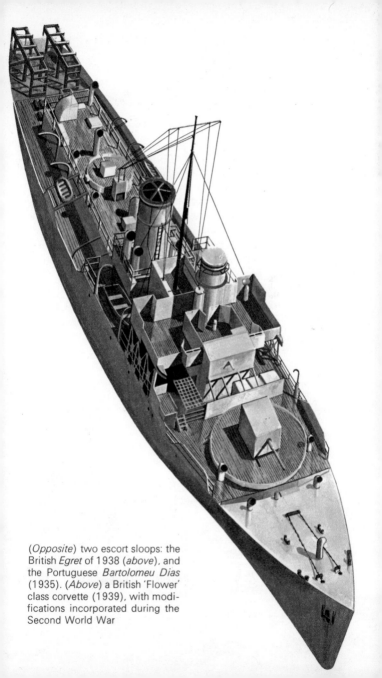

(*Opposite*) two escort sloops: the British *Egret* of 1938 (*above*), and the Portuguese *Bartolomeu Dias* (1935). (*Above*) a British 'Flower' class corvette (1939), with modifications incorporated during the Second World War

and the vessels were completed as either anti-submarine ('Loch' class) or anti-aircraft ('Bay' class) escorts. The United States Navy did not favour the British corvette or frigate but produced a destroyer escort which was slightly larger and faster than the frigate. Japan had neglected escort vessels before the war and had hurriedly to embark on a war pro-gramme although they were given only a fifth priority after aircraft carriers, submarines, destroyers, and minesweepers. But with American submarines taking a heavy toll of mer-chant shipping, escorts were advanced to fourth, and then second, priority during 1943–4. All except half the final series were diesel-engined vessels capable of $19\frac{1}{2}$ knots and armed with two or three 4·7-inch guns. With the slightly smaller

'Kaitoban' class the odd-numbered vessels were diesel engined for a speed of 16½ knots, but turbines were installed in the even-numbered vessels – owing to the shortage of diesel engines – and they were a knot faster.

The modern frigate

At the close of the war there was such a variety of smaller warships that some form of rationalization was inevitable. The frigate category had been universally accepted and destroyer escorts and escort sloops could logically be included in it. The minesweeping sloop was phased out because technical advances with mining had made moored contact mines almost obsolete, and a small non-magnetic and silent craft was now required to deal with non-contact ground mines.

The destroyer also became obsolete as its attacking power – the torpedo and high speed – was of little use against the new capital ship, the aircraft carrier. Although destroyer-type vessels were still built, they were basically fast anti-submarine and anti-aircraft escorts for the fleet, and the speed advantage was the main difference between them and the frigate.

(*Above*) the British frigate *Londonderry* (1961). (*Below*) the Danish frigate *Peder Skram* (1967), powered by gas turbines and diesel engines

The medium-speed frigate was first threatened by the conventionally powered fast submarine, and then completely outpaced by the nuclear submarine, so that a new type of frigate with destroyer speed was required. As an interim measure, until the new generation of fast frigates with sufficient speed to counter nuclear submarines was in service, many destroyers were converted to frigates. To keep size down the first new units were built for specialized roles – for anti-submarine, anti-aircraft, or aircraft-directing duties – and were intended to form self-supporting groups. But as the numbers that could be built were so restricted this policy was later reversed and the general purpose frigate was introduced.

Frigates increased in size to accommodate a missile armament, more sophisticated weaponry and complex electronics (radar, communications, missile test equipment, etc.); they were finally nuclear powered in the United States Navy to accompany the nuclear-powered carrier *Enterprise*. The frigate became so complex and expensive that the pendulum started to swing the other way, and the tendency today is to revert to a frigate that is cheaper, easier and quicker to build. The gas

Two missile-armed frigates: (*above*) the American nuclear-powered *Bainbridge* (1962) and (*below*) the French *Suffren* (1966)

turbine is a great help here, and in 1968 the Royal Navy commissioned the first all-gas turbine frigate, the *Exmouth*.

As a result of experience with the *Exmouth* the Royal Navy decided to adopt all-gas turbine (COGOG) propulsion for frigates and bypass the CODOG (combined diesel engines or gas turbines) installation fitted in foreign contemporaries. Two types of frigates are envisaged to meet future requirements: the more sophisticated type 42 and the less complex type 21. The former has a long-range missile system with matching radar, while the latter has a close-range missile system and therefore does not require such elaborate radar.

Paradoxically, the technically advanced United States Navy is still fitting steam turbines in its escort vessels, but its next series – for which design details have yet to be settled – will almost certainly incorporate gas turbines.

The modern corvette

A small, modern, but basically unsophisticated, vessel, well able to cope with conventional warfare, and generally not exceeding 1,000 tons, has been developed in recent years. Termed a corvette, this craft was diesel engined and, with active fin

stabilization, could continue to operate in heavy weather. Its development is the result of two factors: the number of emergent countries and new navies – all lacking the technical experience and personnel to man sophisticated frigates – and the general need for a 'policing' craft which can be used in minor disturbances where sophisticated weaponry would be out of place. A typical example of the latter was the Indonesian confrontation with Malaysia, when Royal Navy ships sent to that area were all equipped with manually-operated 20-millimetre guns despite the fact they were armed with missiles and fully-automatic guns.

Modern Soviet escort vessels generally fall into this category, and on such a limited displacement can hardly incorporate advanced anti-submarine detection or weapon systems, or face prolonged ocean service.

In a cycle of development that started with gunboats and sloops and finished with frigates and corvettes, it soon becomes apparent that many old strategic ideas have been proved basically sound despite the technical revolution, and that in the final analysis it is always the men, and never the material, that really matter.

Corvettes: (*above*) the Italian *Albatros* (1955) and (*below*) the Ghanaian *Keta* (1966); both are diesel-engined vessels.

MISCELLANEOUS VESSELS

From time to time the orderly progress of warship development was disrupted by the unconventional craft, which either influenced mainstream design or remained an 'original'. Some of these interesting vessels are described here.

The circular ironclad

Designed by the Russian Navy to protect Nikolaiev and the mouth of the River Dnieper, this Black Sea fleet vessel was made circular because no other hull form could have enclosed so great a displacement on the essential limited draught.

The prototype *Novgorod* had a flat-bottomed hull with a diameter of 101 feet and a draught of $13\frac{1}{4}$ feet for a displacement of 2,491 tons. Although the freeboard at the side was only $1\frac{3}{4}$ feet, the deck was cambered so that it was 5 feet at the centre where there was a circular barbette containing two slide-mounted 11-inch breech-loading guns. The hull was protected by a belt varying from 7 inches at the lower edge to 9 inches at the upper edge, a $2\frac{3}{4}$-inch deck, and 9-inch armour on the barbette.

On trials the *Novgorod* attained about 8 knots. She proved unmanageable in a river while going with the current, but behaved better when stemming the current or in open, calm water. However, the type was an overall failure, proving that manoeuvrable, sea-going craft required a shipshape form.

The Russian circular gunboat *Novgorod* (1873)

The British ram *Polyphemus*
(1882)

The British torpedo ram *Polyphemus*

The *Polyphemus* was first conceived with the ram as her only weapon. However, the design was later modified to incorporate submerged torpedo tubes and a few quick-firing guns.

The hull was cylindrical with the curve slightly flattened above water and brought to a point at the keel; the ends were also brought to a point. With a displacement of 2,640 tons she had dimensions of 240(pp) × 40 × 20 feet with only $4\frac{1}{2}$ feet of freeboard amidships. The hull was protected by 3-inch plate carried to a depth of 6 feet below the water-line, and the conning tower and casings for the funnel and ventilators were similarly armoured. There was a light casing on the fore-deck, which extended back to the conning tower and supported the wheelhouse and chartroom, and a hurricane deck for stowing boats. A speed of 17 knots was realized with a total output of 5,500 ihp.

Only one vessel similar to the *Polyphemus* was ever built, and that was the American ram *Katahdin* (ex-*Ammen*) some fifteen years later, but neither ever found general acceptance.

The river gunboat

During the period of colonial expansion, increasing support was given to the army in the field by naval units making the widest possible use of rivers. Although ordinary small warships could navigate the mouths and lower reaches of most rivers, special craft were required for the upper reaches.

Only a flat bottom could provide the necessary shallow draught, and the earliest river gunboats were little better than

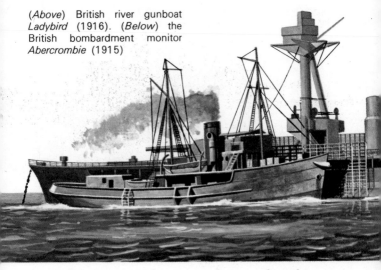

(*Above*) British river gunboat *Ladybird* (1916). (*Below*) the British bombardment monitor *Abercrombie* (1915)

powered pontoons with accommodation and machinery arranged on deck and light guns on the superstructure.

During the First World War the Royal Navy ordered twenty-four river gunboats – twelve large and twelve small – for service in the Middle East. The large vessels – the 'Insect' class – displaced 645 tons, had dimensions of 230(pp)/237½(oa) × 36 × 8½ feet (depth), drew only 4 feet, and had two 6-inch and two 12-pounder guns equally disposed fore and aft.

The British bombardment monitor

The Germans extended the western flank of their army to the coast on their advance through Belgium in 1914, and the Royal Navy rapidly assumed a traditional role in harrying this seaward flank in support of the Allied armies. It used four spare twin 14-inch gun turrets as the basis for a new type of shore bombardment vessel inaptly classed as a monitor.

As shallow draught was essential the hull could not be made deep, and the turret and barbette therefore projected conspicuously above the upper-deck. Abaft the turret was a small bridge structure with the fire control equipment carried at the head of a tall tripod mast used for long-range spotting. Although armour was applied to the turret and barbette, and

armoured bulkheads were provided fore and aft, the side was left unprotected except for a deep anti-torpedo bulge.

Even before they were completed the usefulness of the 14-inch gun monitors was very evident and, when four twin 15-inch turrets were made available, four other units were rushed to completion. Further monitor classes, armed with guns from old battleships and cruisers, were later built.

Coast defence ships

In the pre-dreadnought era the minor navies built battleships smaller than those possessed by the great maritime powers, principally on the grounds of cost. But another reason was that their craft were intended solely for coastal defence and could therefore sacrifice both speed and radius. However, after the *Dreadnought* (see page 20), little cost could be saved with coastal diminutives, and the type became obsolete.

Only three groups of coast defence ships were completed after the *Dreadnought*: the Swedish 'Sverige' class, Finnish 'Väinämöinen' class, and Siamese 'Dhonburi' class.

The Swedish vessels were fast, well protected and a worthy match for the German armoured ship *Deutschland* which was so widely acclaimed a few years later. The Finnish

ships were a remarkable combination of size and power, had a well-disposed secondary dual-purpose battery, and adopted diesel-electric propulsion. The tonnage limitation on the Siamese ships was too severe for them to compare favourably; they were rather short for the weights carried but, with diesel engines, had a good radius of action.

The Swedish multi-purpose craft *Gotland*

This vessel was completed in 1934 as a replacement for the cruiser *Fylgia* (1907) and the minelayer *Klas Fleming* (1914), and, as she was also fitted to operate eleven aircraft, the *Gotland* was one of the most versatile warships ever built.

The flush-decked hull was protected by a deep belt and an armoured deck. The main gun armament was carried in

(*Above*) Finnish coast defence ship *Väinämöinen* (1932). (*Below*) the *Gotland* (1934), a multi-purpose cruiser/seaplane carrier/minelayer

two twin turrets and two single casements on each side of the bridge, while mines were stowed on the main-deck and were conventionally laid through stern ports. Aircraft were stowed on the flight-deck aft and, by a system of rails, were moved forward to the training catapult from which they could be launched at two-minute intervals.

On dimensions of $426\frac{1}{2}$(pp)/443(oa) × $50\frac{1}{4}$ × $16\frac{1}{2}$ feet the *Gotland* had a standard displacement of 4,750 tons, and attained a speed of $27\frac{1}{2}$ knots with a two-shaft geared turbine installation of 33,000 shp.

The fast minelayer

Despite the importance of minelaying few ships are ever built specifically for this role. Therefore, two surprising

features of the British 1938 and 1939 Naval Programmes were the provision of four minelayers – the 'Abdiel' class – and the high speed with which they were endowed.

On a displacement of 2,650 tons these vessels had dimensions of $400\frac{1}{2}$(pp)/418(oa) $\times$ 40 $\times$ $11\frac{1}{2}$ feet and were flush decked with the greater part of the main-deck aft used to stow 160 mines. They were powered by two sets of geared turbines developing 72,000 shp for a speed of 39 knots, and were armed with 4·7-inch guns in twin mountings fore and aft, controlled by a director on the bridge: sufficient to ward off attacks by destroyers, the only vessels fast enough to challenge them.

The Japanese torpedo cruisers *Oi* and *Kitakami*

In 1933 the Imperial Japanese Navy introduced the type 93 oxygen-fuelled 24-inch torpedo (the 'Long Lance') which had a range of 43,500 yards at 36 knots and a 1,100-pound warhead. This weapon, which completely outclassed the standard 21-inch torpedo in other navies, was fitted to all new cruiser and destroyer construction, and to many earlier cruisers and destroyers.

Two light cruisers, the *Oi* and *Kitakami*, were completely rearmed in 1941 when they were fitted with five quintuple banks of 24-inch torpedo tubes on each side amidships; the sides were sponsoned out to provide the appropriate training arcs. No other warship ever equalled the torpedo armament carried by these two vessels. The gun armament was reduced to four 5·5-inch (later 5-inch anti-aircraft) weapons in open twin mountings fore and aft, but the light anti-aircraft armament was considerably reinforced to comprise thirty-six 25-millimetre guns (six triple shields and eighteen single mounts).

Combatant naval auxiliaries

All navies have drawn on their mercantile marines during hostilities to supplement the ships and personnel of the fighting fleets; but the combatant value of naval auxiliaries has diminished as warships become more sophisticated. In the Second World War the conversion to aircraft carriers and anti-aircraft vessels provided the most combatant auxiliary vessels.

The former cross-channel passenger ferry *Ulster Queen* was extensively altered to ship an anti-aircraft armament of six 4-inch guns in three twin mountings, eight 2-pounders in two quadruple mountings and ten single 20-millimetre guns; she was provided with a high-angle director aft, air warning radar at the mastheads, and surface warning radar on the bridge.

But the most significant conversions were undertaken by the Imperial Japanese Navy, which turned seven passenger liners into aircraft carriers. Although these vessels lacked the speed and protection of the full fleet carriers they nevertheless proved valuable additions to attack groups.

(*Opposite*) the Japanese torpedo cruiser *Kitakami*, converted in 1941. (*Below*) the British mine-layer *Abdiel* (1941)

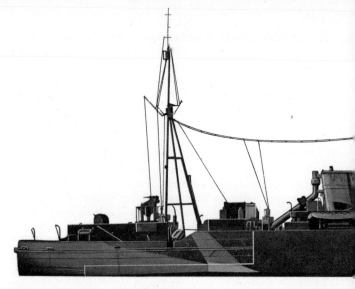

The paddle aircraft carrier

During the Second World War United States naval pilots desperately needed to practise deck landings on a training carrier. With shipbuilding capacity fully extended the vessels were converted from two excursion paddle steamers, and commissioned as the *Wolverine* and *Sable*. Their superstructures were dismantled and a flight-deck, overhanging the bow and stern, was built over the existing hull. As hangars were not provided the flight-deck was close to the water-line, and aircraft landed and took off with the minimum interval.

(*Above*) the British auxiliary anti-aircraft ship *Ulster Queen*, converted in 1941. (*Below*) the American training carrier *Wolverine,* which was converted in 1942, with side paddle propulsion

The tank landing craft

After the conquest of Europe in 1940 the British services realized that the occupied countries would be liberated only by a massive assault from the sea, but special craft were required to land the heavy, bulky equipment used by modern armies in the field. Owing to the relatively short sea distances involved, small craft could be used and the basic requirements were outlined as (a) simple construction for rapid production; (b) ability to beach and therefore a shallow draught so that vehicles would not have to be specially waterproofed; and (c) a bow ramp to ease off-loading. The craft for both troops (assault landing craft or LCAs) and equipment (tank landing craft or LCTs) differed only in size.

The British tank landing craft Mk. 1 (LCT [1]) was designed to carry three 40-ton tanks, and tank-deck size determined the craft's dimensions of $135(pp)/151\frac{1}{4}(oa) \times 29 \times 3(fwd)/5\frac{3}{4}(aft)$ feet. As the bow ramp needed a bluff bow there was no question of high speed, and two diesel engines, totalling 1,000 bhp, gave 10 knots. The bridge, limited accommodation, and machinery were all located aft, and a purely defensive armament of two light (2-pounder or 20-millimetre) anti-aircraft guns was mounted in the bridge wings.

The landing ship tank

Although the performance of the tank landing craft exceeded all expectations, in 1940 Britain still required a vessel that could beach and land a tank anywhere in the world.

The British Admiralty plan for such a vessel was outlined to the American authorities and resulted in the popular tank landing ship Mk.2 (LST [2]). As shallow draught and an ocean-going capability were hardly compatible, these vessels were ballasted down for the sea passage and before beaching the tanks were pumped out until the tank-deck was practically parallel with the water-line.

The tank landing ship Mk.2 had a standard displacement of 1,625 tons with dimensions of 316(wl)/327$\frac{3}{4}$(oa) × 50 × 3(fwd)/9$\frac{1}{2}$(aft) feet when trimmed for beaching. It could carry eighteen 30-ton tanks in the tank-deck, one tank landing craft Mk.5 (LCT [5]) or twenty-seven 3-ton lorries and eight jeeps on the upper-deck, and 177 troops. Main propulsion was by diesel engines of 1,800 bhp for a speed of 10 knots, and the armament comprised one 12-pounder and six 20-millimetre anti-aircraft guns.

(*Above*) British tank landing craft *Mk.8* (1945). (*Below*) an American landing ship tank of the 'County' class (1953)

The landing ship dock

This vessel was designed to transport loaded tank landing craft over long distances. Although it duplicated the task of the tank landing ship its design was cast at a time when the tank landing craft was well established, but when tank landing ships were in an early stage of development and appeared unsuitable for series production.

Handling a loaded tank landing craft presented special problems, and the only way it could be loaded and discharged was to lock it in and out of a floating dock structure. Basically, therefore, the landing ship dock was a powered floating dock with a shipshape bow, over which was arranged the bridge and accommodation; the stern was closed by a watertight ramp hinged at the foot. The dock walls housed the boiler and engine rooms, store rooms, ballast tanks and pumping machinery; and further ballast tanks and bunkers were arranged in the double bottom.

The craft had dimensions of 454(pp)/457$\frac{3}{4}$(oa) × 72$\frac{1}{4}$ × 17 feet and a standard displacement of 4,270 tons in sea-going trim, increased to 7,930 tons when loaded and flooded-down.

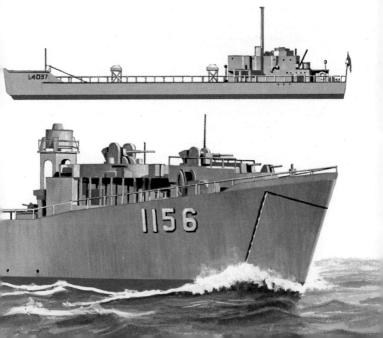

(*Above*) American landing ship dock, 'Thomaston' class (1955). (*Below*) British headquarters ship *Bulolo*, converted in 1942

The headquarters ship

In large-scale combined operations during the Second World War, a prime requirement was the provision of a headquarters ship from which the naval and military commanders could correlate the activities of their widely dispersed units ashore and afloat.

In order not to tie up a major naval unit in such a restrictive role, it was found expedient to equip medium-sized merchant ships with a good turn of speed because they had the necessary space for fitting the wide range of communications equipment required and for accommodating the naval and military staffs. A typical example was the former Australian passenger vessel *Bulolo*, which was first requisitioned by the Royal Navy in 1940 as an armed merchant cruiser. In 1942 she was converted to a headquarters ship and served at the Sicilian, Italian, and Normandy landings. She had dimensions of 399(pp)/412½(oa) × 58¼ × 21½ feet, displaced 9,111 tons and was powered by diesel engines of 6,000 bhp at a speed of 15 knots. Her defensive armament included four 4-inch anti-aircraft guns in two twin mountings, five single 40-millimetre anti-aircraft guns and fourteen single 20-millimetre anti-aircraft guns. She could carry 238 troops and under her davits six personnel landing craft for putting them ashore.

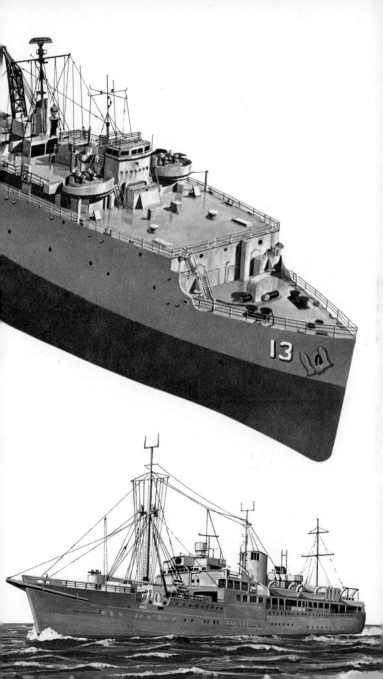

BOOKS TO READ

Two comprehensive series are *Warships of World War II*, published by Ian Allan Ltd, Shepperton, Middlesex, and *Navies of the Second World War*, published by Macdonald & Co., London. These two series between them include books on the warships of all the major powers involved in the war.

An Italian series, *Le Navi d'Italia*, is published by Ufficio Storico della Marina Militare of Rome.

Among the books published by the United States Naval Institute, Annapolis, Maryland, three are of particular interest: *Weyer's Warships of the World* by G. Albrecht; *The Imperial and Royal Austro-Hungarian Navy* by A. Sokol; and *Flush Decks and Four Pipes* by John D. Alden.

The German Navy can be referred to in three books published by J. F. Lehmanns Verlag, Munich: *Die deutschen Krigsschiffe 1815-1945* by E. Gröner; *Weyer's Flottentaschenbuch* by G. Albrecht; and *60 Jahre Deutsche U-Boote 1906-1966* by B. Herzog.

Other books and journals about the modern warship are: *Aircraft Carriers* by N. Polmar, Doubleday, New York; *Almanacco Navale* by G. Giorgerini, Rivista Marittima, Rome; *British Cruisers* (two vols. in preparation) by H. L. Lenton, Ian Allan, Shepperton; *Dictionary of American Naval Fighting Ships* (three vols. and others in preparation), U.S. Government Printing Office, Washington DC; *Dreadnought* by R. Hough, Allen & Unwin, London; *Flottes de Combat* by H. Le Masson, Editions Maritimes et d'Outre-Mer, Paris; *Imperial Japanese Navy 1865-1945* by A. J. Watts and B. Gordon, Macdonald, London; *Naval Record* (bi-monthly journal), Monitor (Naval Publications) Ltd, London; *Royal Fleet Auxiliary* by E. E. Sigwart, Adlard Coles, London; *Send a Gunboat* by A. Preston and I. Major, Longmans, London; *Warship International* (quarterly journal), R.A.A.P., Radford, Virginia; *Warships of the British and Commonwealth Navies* by H. T. Lenton, Ian Allan, Shepperton.

ABBREVIATIONS EXPLAINED

Two groups of abbreviations mentioned in the text may be unfamiliar to the reader. Three relate to ship dimensions:–

oa	overall length
pp	perpendicular length
wl	water-line

and three to horse-power:–

bhp	brake horse-power
ihp	indicated horse-power
shp	shaft horse-power

INDEX

157

SOME OTHER TITLES IN THIS SERIES